ANY BOY CAN

ANY BOY CAN

THE ARCHIE MOORE STORY

by
Archie Moore
and
Leonard B. Pearl

PRENTICE-HALL, INC., Englewood Cliffs, N.J.

ANY BOY CAN: The Archie Moore Story
By Archie Moore and Leonard B. Pearl
Copyright © 1971 by Archie Lee Moore and Leonard B. Pearl

ISBN 0-13-038562-X
Library of Congress Catalog Card Number: 76-163398
Printed in the United States of America   •   *T*

Prentice-Hall International, Inc., London
Prentice-Hall of Australia, Pty. Ltd., Sydney
Prentice-Hall of Canada, Ltd., Toronto
Prentice-Hall of India Private Ltd., New Delhi
Prentice-Hall of Japan, Inc., Tokyo

To JOAN MOORE *and* FLORENCE PEARL, *two wonderful wives who take their marriage vows seriously.*

ACKNOWLEDGMENTS

To our agent, C. M. Vandeburg, of Vandeburg-Linkletter Associates for his encouragement and valuable suggestions.

To Director Louis Lake and all the great Any Boy Can boys for their cooperation.

To the many famous personalities who were kind enough to write to me and tell me their personal thoughts about Archie Moore.

To relatives and friends who encouraged us to do this book.

It is our sincere wish that this book, besides being exciting, enlightening, inspirational and entertaining, accomplish two important purposes. We hope that it will prove that any boy can succeed if he wants to and receives a little help, thus motivating him to lead a happier and more productive life; and we hope that it will promote harmony, freedom and equality among all races and religions.

ARCHIE MOORE
LEONARD PEARL

FOREWORD

Almost everybody knows that Archie Moore held the world's light-heavyweight boxing championship. Many others know that he held that title for ten years, finally retiring undefeated. But very few people know what he had to go through to achieve it. And that is what part of this book is all about. It is the inspiring story of a man who rose from the depths to the heights because of his courage, determination and faith. It is the story of his frustrations and bitter disappointments, the hard work and danger, the years of being penniless and hungry before Archie Moore, the Magnificent Mongoose, destroyed his opponents in the ring like the mongoose of India destroys rats and snakes.

The other part of this story is about Archie Moore the humanitarian, a man dedicated to family, God and country, to helping the underprivileged, to helping mold the youth of America so that they can live better lives and become better citizens of the greatest country in the world.

I have been asked if Archie is militant, so I looked the word up in the dictionary. One definition is that a militant is an aggressive person, a fighter. Certainly he is aggressive, and certainly he is a fighter. But he is fighting for

all the good things—and he is fighting in a nonviolent and
constructive way. What's wrong with that?

Archie Moore attracted global attention when he
wrote an open letter denouncing violence after the Detroit riots. The United States Information Agency felt it
important enough to distribute reprints to its offices for
republication in English and foreign languages, and it has
been quoted four times in the Congressional Record and
reprinted in many leading newspapers. In the letter, Archie said:

> The devil is at work in America and it's up to
> us to drive him out. Those who would profit
> from their brother's misfortune, and those who
> would set fellow Americans upon each other
> deserve no mercy.
>
> Granted the Negro still has a long way to go
> to get a fair shake. But believe this, if we resort
> to violence and lawlessness we will lose every-
> thing.

Archie, of course, is for civil rights. He is for civil rights
with all his heart and all his soul. He wants equality and
justice for the black people as well as for all minority
groups, but he does not feel that civil rights demonstra-
tions give anyone license to burn, loot, kill and steal. He
feels very deeply the past and present injustices suffered
by the black people, and occasionally he sounds off about
his feelings. Nevertheless, he still believes that civil rights
can be accomplished by nonviolent, constructive means,
and in this book he discloses how this can be accomplished and what he is doing to help so that all people can
live together in peace and harmony.

However, as much as Archie Moore and many other

people want civil rights to come about in a peaceful manner, I think it would be wise for those who oppose racial equality to think over the following quote by President John F. Kennedy: "Those who make peaceful revolution impossible will make the violent revolution inevitable."

Although there is a tough road ahead, Archie's work is beginning to receive recognition. A recent letter to me from Mr. James Keogh, Special Assistant to President Nixon, read: "You can be sure he [President Nixon] shares your very high regard for Mr. Moore and the outstanding work he is doing in behalf of our youth."

In 1968, Governor Reagan wrote Archie: "I most certainly agree with you that ABC is a positive step in the right direction. I was glad to see you here in Sacramento recently and can assure you that we are going to do all in our power to help meet the needs in our communities."

In 1969, Governor Reagan stated: "The depth of compassion for the youth of our country as exemplified by Archie Moore should be an inspiration to men of all colors and creeds."

Senator George Murphy hailed Archie as a Californian who has done a truly magnificent job with youngsters. "Everyone in Washington was tremendously impressed with the wonderful work Mr. Moore has done with the Any Boy Can program," Senator Murphy stated as he praised the precepts taught in the ABC program, particularly the one urging students to remain in school. On another occasion, Senator Murphy said: "Archie Moore, a former world's champion light-heavyweight boxer, won the plaudits of the sports world for his performances and decency in the ring. Since leaving it, he has become an exemplary citizen, working for his country's best interests."

On September 10, 1969, Senator Murphy had the following entered in the Congressional Record:

> Mr. President, one of my close friends and fellow Californians, Archie Moore, former light-heavyweight champion, is engaged in a vital and praiseworthy battle which is as challenging as any he faced during his long career in the ring. This battle is to save youths from a life of juvenile delinquency and push them in the right direction so that they may become productive and successful citizens of our country. His own city is as proud of him and his work as he is of San Diego. Certainly, this is a kind of program that deserves more attention and support. I ask unanimous consent that two articles praising Archie Moore be printed at this point in the Record.

There was no objection, and the articles were printed in the Congressional Record.

A letter from Representative Robert L. Leggett said:

> The dramatic impact of Archie Moore's program was never more obvious than when he started his pilot project in Vallejo, California. In a matter of weeks, the major poverty and slum area of this community became a model of civic pride.
>
> The instant results provided by this program, pride in family, pride in self, and pride in community and church, launched a clean up, paint your house, mow your lawn campaign the likes of which had never before been seen. Vandalism practically came to a standstill, grades in school improved, teachers were surprised by the new and enthusiastic attitude that students exposed to ABC displayed.

This simple program, invented if you will, by this devoted man with built-in character, who believes that God and country come first, and that honesty is born in every man, has literally worked miracles in my home town, and can do the same in yours. . . . ABC: Any Boy Can.

A letter from Representative Lionel Van Deerlin read:

I am delighted to learn that a book on the life of Archie Moore is nearing completion. Even had I not been a San Diegan, I could not have helped being a long-time admirer of Archie.

His achievements in the ring have of course stamped him as one of the greatest fighters of all times—a man to rank with the legendary all-time greats. As a fighter, he showed himself to be a man of compassion, surely a paradoxical trait in one whose chief objective is to overwhelm an opponent by physical force and skill. But Archie demonstrated this trait in full measure in the sportsmanlike manner in which he conducted his bouts and his treatment of beaten adversaries.

This spirit of compassion, this regard for his fellow man, and particularly for youth, has been demonstrated even more forceably since he left the ring. I am well aware of his efforts in behalf of boys of all ages, all races and all creeds, and of his untiring efforts on their behalf. His program, "Any Boy Can," is nationally known, and Archie deservedly received praise from the highest quarters for his work.

I look forward with eagerness and anticipation to reading the book. Archie Moore can and should stand as an inspiration to every youth,

athlete and non-athlete alike, and I know that
the book will help to make known his image
and his accomplishments to thousands for
whom he will be such an inspiration.

Representative Van Deerlin also had Archie's statement on "Operation Gardener" entered in the Congressional Record. Van Deerlin said:

This is a remarkable statement on interracial
relations by a most remarkable San Diegan. His
recommendations deserve close study at the
highest levels of government, for he knows
whereof he speaks. This great champion is no
Uncle Tom, but neither, on the other hand,
does he harbor any sympathy for the racial extremists who seek to divide our nation.

In Archie's "Operation Gardener," Archie had said in
part:

Do we have to choke what could be a beautiful garden with weeds of hate? I say no, and I
stand ready to start "Operation Gardener." I invite the respected black leaders of our country
to join me. Lawlessness and violence will not
help the blacks achieve equality with the white
man. As a starting point for interracial cooperation, I offer my Any Boy Can Program, which
also is a juvenile delinquency deterrent, a youth
motivation program and an aid to disadvantaged boys in achieving the better things in life,
all in one ball of wax.

Archie expressed the views of many, both black and
white, when he said that the answer to the blacks' prob-

lems was not in rioting, but in taking advantage of more opportunities he felt the white man has a duty to provide.

"Don't talk to me of your 'guaranteed income,'" Archie said. "Any fool knows that this is insanity. The world owes nobody—black or white—a living. God helps those who help themselves."

Senator Alan Cranston said: "Archie Moore is surely to be commended for his efforts to help disadvantaged youngsters find goals and satisfaction in their lives."

Senator Charles H. Percy wrote: "I was most pleased to read of the outstanding work that Archie Moore is doing to bring inner-city boys, particularly young blacks, into the scouting movement. The ABC program is certainly one of the more worthwhile programs for young people today."

A letter from Mr. Norman Knight in behalf of Senator Edward M. Kennedy read: "The Senator wants you to know how much he admires Archie Moore's objectives of achieving racial harmony and motivating American Youth to become good, productive citizens."

Congressman L. Mendel Rivers wrote:

> You don't know how happy I am to hear from you. You happen to be one of my favorites. Every night I thank God for what you are doing for the young people of America, particularly the promising black youth of this great country.
>
> I want you to always remember that you have my prayers, and that I'm as close as your telephone.
>
> May the Lord bless you and keep you and give you the strength to continue the magnificent work you are doing for America.

San Diego's Mayor Frank Curran said:

The City of San Diego has many reasons to be grateful to and proud of Mr. Archie Moore, and I am pleased to learn that you are collaborating in publishing a book on Mr. Moore's life relating his long and impressive record as one of the outstanding ring champions of all time.

It has been my privilege as a city councilman and as Mayor of the City of San Diego to work closely with Mr. Moore during the past fourteen years. He is highly regarded by the entire community for his unfailing promotion of good sportsmanship, and most recently, his unreserved contribution of time and energy to the youth of our city and country; and specifically, his current ABC program, which everyone knows stands for Any Boy Can.

I will certainly look forward to reading this book.

Congressman Bob Wilson wrote: "I thought you would like to have a few copies of the Republican Congressional Committee's *Newsletter* which carried the article on your ABC Program.

"We're very proud of the fine work you have been doing with these young boys and am sure your program will be turning out some great Americans."

Richard L. Vaughn, presiding judge of the juvenile department of the California Superior Court, wrote:

My son and I were present at the Silver Gate elementary school PTA father-son annual meeting last week when you put on the program which consisted of one of your fight films, the participation of your sons and some students of the ABC Club.

I am writing this letter, not only in the capacity of being your friend for over thirty years, but also as Presiding Judge of the Juvenile Court, to thank you for your contribution in time and effort to the youth of San Diego, and even more important, for what you will contribute in the future. I know that every boy that listened to you and was involved and participated in your program from the audience and from the stage, cannot help but be a better boy. They will remember the evening's entertainment for many years.

Again, good luck on your program, and I hope that the building program for the Boys' Club is a success. If I can be of any help to you in counseling any of your students, please feel free to call upon me.

General Westmoreland stated: "Your campaign to stamp out juvenile delinquency is truly commendable. Your continued support is appreciated."

A letter from General Eugene A. Salet, Commandant of the U. S. Army War College, read: "Thanks for sending me the information on your ABC program. This is great work you are doing. Keep it up. Your reward is in knowing that you are developing boys into men who will be a source of pride to this nation. You know that you have my best wishes for the successful continuation of your work."

Colonel John Prodan, United States Air Force, said: "I think that yours is the solution to this problem that faces our country. I can only hope that it spreads."

Judge John J. Purchio, Presiding Judge of the Juvenile Court of Alameda County, stated: "As a Juvenile Court Judge, I feel that this kind of program [ABC], with your guidance and tutelage, should be instituted on a much wider scale throughout our State."

Hubert H. Humphrey, former Vice President, stated: "Unquestionably, the lending of your fine name to such a program would do much to assuring its ultimate success."

Chief of Police Jack Stiltz of Vallejo, said: "In my opinion Archie Moore's ABC program is a well-rounded, character-building and body-conditioning program for all youth. Not only does Archie teach young boys the value of keeping fit and the art of self-defense, but also at the same time he teaches them spiritual values, clean living, high moral standards, fair play, self-respect and respect for authority."

Last, but by no means least, is this comment by Captain E. Robert Anderson, Editor Emiritus of the Copley Newspapers and a good friend of Archie:

"If some bigot can misguide, then I can guide."

With that statement from Archie Moore, 8 August 1967, I was suddenly aware that the United States of America had a new champion, this time in the greater arena of the welfare of a nation and all its people.

I had known Archie for many years and admired him as a sportsman and compassionate friend. He was fiercely intent as a crusader that August day when he walked into our newspaper offices with a sincerity of purpose requiring immediate attention. And he got it through the front page of the *San Diego Union* and the challenging caption "Guide or Misguide."

It was a message reprinted throughout the country and heard on television and radio countless times.

The nation was reeling from a series of foul blows but Archie was in there punching at the crucial moment.

Let's never forget Archie's words of wisdom in 1967. He spoke wisely with:

"I was born in a ghetto but I refused to stay there. I am a Negro and proud to be one. I am also an American and proud of that.

"Hate is bait . . . bait for the simple-minded.

"If we resort to lawlessness, the only thing we can hope for is civil war, untold bloodshed and end of our dreams."

Surely Archie was restating for Abraham Lincoln needs of the times when the Great Emancipator called upon us "with malice toward none; with charity for all; with firmness in the right, as God gives us to see the right, let us strive on to finish the work we are in; to bind up the nation's wounds. . . ."

Leonard Pearl

ONE

•

In 1962 I hung up my gloves after a match with Cassius
Clay, now known as Muhammad Ali. I knew long before
this that Clay was going to be a great fighter, probably
one of the greatest heavyweights of all time, but for a
while it looked like he wouldn't have a chance to prove
it.

I actually helped to train Clay and taught him for three
months, you see. When he came out of the Olympics he
had one pro fight in Texas, which he won by a knockout.
His managers brought him to me right here in San Diego
and wanted me to train him. So I did, and I didn't want a
contract with the boy, because I felt that if we could get
along, we didn't need a contract. I've always been one of
these guys who felt that a man's word is his bond, and if
he likes you, well, you didn't need a contract. We worked
together, and Clay showed me a lot, an awful lot, in the
area of speed.

Clay seemed to me like a very affable man—affable
boy at the time, he was only nineteen years old—and
then as he progressed and began to learn things, he began
to demand more and more teaching. I really wanted to
take my time and teach him a lot of real solid things that
would make him impregnable as a heavyweight cham-

pion. I knew he was going to be the champion one day, but I had no idea he was going to make it so soon.

The reason I fought him in 1962 was not because of me wanting to fight him or trying to prove something, you understand. After all, I was almost fifty years old at the time, and no man that age belongs in the same ring with a youngster in his prime, especially one who had Clay's great talent. I was just fighting him because I had some paper hung on me, in the vernacular of the ring. A promoter had hung a $25,000 check on me that bounced. I had to make it good, and my money was tied up in my house and so on, and I had to come up with ready cash, and the quickest way I could get cash was to fight Clay. So I boxed him. I felt that if I could put together all the things I had learned in my many years in the ring that I stood a good chance of beating him in spite of the age difference, but he was just too much.

A lot of times I've been asked how I thought I would have done against Clay when I was in my prime. Well, truly, the only way I can answer that is to say I don't honestly know. I always went into the ring feeling that I could beat my opponent, but it didn't always happen that way. One thing I can tell you for sure—it would have been an interesting and exciting fight.

I left the ring with mixed feelings—it was like leaving a part of me behind; yet I was eager and anxious to go ahead on a full-time basis with my youth work. I was looking forward to it with the great anticipation generated by many years of planning. But twenty-nine years of a man's life aren't just dumped that easily, you know, and I had so many memories that when I thought of having left the ring forever it gave me a kind of empty feeling. Even the bad times became fond memories and served to make the good times more enjoyable.

Knowing what a rough time I had, people often ask me if I feel that it has all been worth it. I remember the first time I was asked that question, and my thoughts went way, way back, and I visualized the sad, lonely days when hardly anybody knew who Archie Moore was. I was just another name in small print on a fight card—just another black kid spilling his blood to make a few bucks to stay alive in the hope that there were better days ahead. I would fight for short money in little towns; then, my body still clammy with sweat because the little arena had no showers and I couldn't afford a hotel room, I would ride a dusty, dirty bus or freight train to the next town, still hurting and bruised from my last fight. And I thought of the filthy rat- and bug-infested two-bit flophouses I had to stay in; and the cheap, starchy foods eaten in crummy little restaurants; and I thought of even leaner days when I didn't have a cent in my pocket, and I was so hungry and cold and tired that even the cheap food and dirty flophouses would have been as welcome as a life preserver to a drowning man. It would have been like living at the Ritz and having a thick, juicy steak for dinner. Many times it seemed like the security of a nine-to-five job would have been better, even if it was as a janitor or dishwasher. But I was determined to become a champion regardless of the cost, and eventually boxing was real good to me, and after weighing the pros and cons the answer is quite obvious.

Becoming champion created a new world for me, and when asked whether or not I would do it all over again, or whether it was worth that much to me, I say I would, because it seemed to give me an experience that I would never have been able to get, even with a college degree or in another profession, because it put me in hand-to-hand contact with people of great stature. And as time

went by I settled myself into these high states. I became
accustomed to living a much better life. I adjusted readily
and began to communicate with people. I began to learn
their idioms—how they talked, how they acted, how they
ate, how they reacted to certain things. It was a brand-
new experience for me, and I feel that it was all worth it
—even the hard knocks, because life's road is not always
smooth. And surely my rugged road was very interesting
and very rewarding at the end.

And at the end, the culmination of winning the championship of the world gave me a new platform on which
to base an argument that youth should be served quite
early in helping them to shape their lives, to change their
attitudes or establish good attitudes, and this is the way
that young people should be able to step off in life—with
their best foot forward.

And becoming champion of the world was tangible
proof that I was doing a good job in my chosen profession, you understand. This knowledge that they are doing
a good job is important for everybody, no matter what
their job is—bricklayer, bookkeeper, housewife or whatever. And becoming top man in my division was important to me because it fulfilled a need everybody has—the
need to feel important. And it's the desire to feel important that motivates people to do great things. It's nice
being recognized. It makes you feel good when somebody
asks you for your autograph, and any of these personalities who complain about people who ask them for their
autographs would feel pretty bad if the fans stopped asking them.

And winning the championship was also the fulfillment
of a dream. And it's nice to have dreams come true. Winning the championship was important, but I feel that
what I am doing now is much more important, because

trying to help young people gain confidence in the society which has somehow neglected them, and trying to make them aware that there are spiritual values, you know, is of prime importance. Making them aware that there is an Almighty by relating what had happened to me. I believe that there is something greater than all of us—and that is the God that is willing to help us, you see. We can't deny that. I'm not kidding myself. I couldn't have accomplished what I did without God's help. He allowed me to become a champion, and I'm deeply grateful, and now I want to show Him my gratitude by helping others. I feel that I'm building something—that I'm building on something. I know that this could mean the difference in attitudes in many areas, because people with negative attitudes, they never amount to anything, so we try to change their attitude to a positive one.

I know from my own experiences. For example, there were many times that I had a negative attitude caused by disappointments and frustrations. But I forced myself to change my attitude and keep trying. I remember back in 1949 I had built up an impressive record but still hadn't been able to get a crack at the championship. I had fought and beaten the best in Australia, and had fought the best in America, traveling from the West Coast to the East Coast and all whistle stops in between, and my only losses during the preceding three years had been to Ezzard Charles, a heavyweight who somehow had me hexed, and to Len Morrow, Henry Hall and Lloyd Gibson. The rest of my fights I had won, and many by knockouts, but still I was almost out of money and had no prospects of getting a championship fight, although most sportswriters and fans agreed that I was entitled to a chance, you see. So I thought I would quit the ring game and go back home, but then I became determined to change my attitude to a positive one, and I worked harder than ever. I subbed for Bob Satterfield and fought the Alabama Kid in Toledo. He knocked me down in the first round, but I got up and knocked him down four times in the third round and then knocked him out in the fourth.

The papers played the victory up big, and the next thing I knew I was matched against Bob Satterfield, and I knocked him out in the third round on January 31, 1949, in Toledo. Then I knocked the Alabama Kid out again, and followed this with knockouts over Dusty Wilkerson and Jimmy Bivins, and I was on my way again.

I won 29 of my next 31 fights—22 by knockouts and 7 by decisions. This carried me into 1952, and my record forced the fight with Joey Maxim, whom I beat for the light-heavyweight championship on December 17, 1952. During the span between the Bivins and Maxim fights, I had lost only two fights, to Clint Bacon and Harold Johnson and later beat both of these men. So you see the importance of a positive attitude and keeping on trying.

This was again demonstrated in 1954. I was the light-heavyweight champion, but I was discouraged and disgusted with boxing and in bad shape financially. The big money was to be made in fighting the top heavyweights, you see, and just as I had a tough time getting to fight Maxim for the light-heavyweight title, I was having an equally tough time getting a crack at the heavyweight title. I was again thinking about quitting the ring, but then, encouraged by some friends, I started a publicity campaign that eventually got me the heavyweight championship fight with Rocky Marciano.

I'm often asked if I'm bitter about these things that happened to me, but believe this: I'm not at all bitter and I don't hate anybody. Because why? Well, when you are bitter and hate, you are only hurting yourself. Bitterness and hatred are self-destructive emotions. Any doctor will tell you the great mental and physical damage that results when a person has bitterness or hatred in his heart. It is a poison of the worst sort. Only a fool will allow himself to be a victim of bitterness or hate. And anyone who teaches others to hate is poisoning them. Children are born without hate. It is something they are taught. People would be doing their children so much more good if they taught them love instead of hate. You know, the young people can be reached. All they need is for someone to show them the way. We have to teach them the correct moral and spiritual principles, and respect for law and order, if America is to have qualified leaders in the future. We must emphasize patience and patriotism and reverence, and motivate the young, no matter what their race, religion or creed might be. We must emphasize tolerance for other people's beliefs. If we want them to be tolerant of our race, religion or creed, we must be equally tolerant of theirs, you understand. Everyone is entitled to their own beliefs, and they should be respected by others of different beliefs.

I believe in civil rights. This goes without saying, but my battle is not only a civil rights battle. It is a battle for all people in America, and particularly our youth and our underprivileged of all ages. Great social change is sweeping our country, and it is the responsibility of young people everywhere to identify with the change and insure that it is for the good and accomplished in a nonviolent way.

You know, I believe in the Golden Rule: Do unto others as you would have them do unto you. This is beautiful. At night, before I go to bed, it's research time. What did I accomplish today? Whom did I wrong? I try not to

make the same mistake a second time. I would rather
hurt myself than my neighbor, because I know that I can
take it and keep going, and I'm trying to instill these
ideals in the minds of the boys I come in contact with.

We use a word in the Any Boy Can program—"position." It is really a simple word, but it has a solid ring,
and the ABC student who stands neutral, he can't do his
thing. This is the mystic part of ABC, because we give
our message in little mystic statements. Well, "position"
has three syllables, and on the last syllable, which is *shun*,
the youngster finds himself ready and able to protect and
defend his moral and spiritual precepts, and this leads to
that thing we call courage, you see.

Many of the youngsters were sadly lacking in courage
when they joined ABC, but I'll guarantee that they didn't
lack it for long. And this is great, very great. I remember
in 1969 our ABC boys put on a boxing show for the
benefit of multiple sclerosis victims. Here were these underprivileged boys who had so little, gladly doing a
benefit for people they felt were less fortunate than they
because of their illness.

Most of the ABC boys didn't even have any boxing
equipment, so they simply took off their shirts and shoes,
put on the gloves and were ready to go. One event we
held was the battle royal, where five boys go into the ring
at one time. They were to box until only one participant
remained. There was one little white boy and four soul
brothers. The black boys didn't gang up on the white
boy. They were absolutely color blind, as was the mixed
black-and-white audience.

Anyway, after several minutes of nonstop slugging,
there were these two black boys of about equal weight,
height and ability who were left, and they were standing
toe-to-toe, slugging it out. Neither one would give an

inch, and the fans were on their feet at this gutty display. One boy was so tired that tears were streaming down his cheeks, and believe me, it was a sight to behold. Here was this soul brother, arm weary and tired, so tired that he couldn't keep the tears back, but he was still standing his ground, punching and being punched, and he wasn't about to quit.

I'm always proud of these boys, but at times like this I'm especially proud of them, and it makes all the hard work, long hours and money spent really worthwhile. Those twin streams of water running down those black cheeks were badges of courage, but I thought he had had enough, so I turned to him and said, "Do you want to quit?"

"No, sir!" came the emphatic reply.

I asked the other boy if he wanted to quit, and his "No, sir!" was just as emphatic.

After a few minutes more I asked them if they wanted a draw, but they shook their heads vigorously. But it looked like they would go on and on forever, so I finally called it a draw and the fans went wild, cheering and throwing money in the ring. It was a proud and happy moment for me, and I felt like a surgeon who had done a successful organ transplant. Only, in this case it wasn't an organ but that invaluable thing called courage.

TWO

●

Practically all my life I've felt like a guy trying to climb a glass mountain—I would climb two steps up and then slide four steps back. When I was in boxing I fought many years longer than I should have had to before I got a shot at the light-heavyweight title. And the same thing happened when I went after the heavyweight championship. I scratched and clawed my way up that glass mountain until I could almost touch the peak with my outstretched fingertips. And you know, it was like a bad dream where you're trying to reach something but never can.

I was lucky in that I finally did get to the top of one mountain when I was matched against Joey Maxim and won the light-heavyweight championship. During this climb I was taken advantage of and exploited by both black men and white men. But don't get me wrong—I'm not complaining and I'm not bitter, because I've also been helped by black men and white men. And besides, I felt that there were other and more important glass mountains to climb before I could reach the goals I felt that God had put me on this earth for, and that my problems were part of a plan to prepare me and test me to see if I was worthy.

People often ask me what my toughest fight was—and I know they are asking about the toughest fight I had in the ring—but I always tell them that my toughest fight is right now, because now, you understand, I am fighting for the things that really count: I am fighting to help our youth become happy, productive citizens instead of juvenile delinquents; I am fighting to help the underprivileged of all ages; I am fighting for racial harmony and equality; and I am fighting to make this a better America for all of us. And in my fight I seek help from people of all races and religions; and people of all races and religions *do* help me. Because I associate with white people as well as blacks, I have on occasions been called an Uncle Tom. This is definitely not true. Nobody, but nobody, pulls my chain, and I'll fight any man who says otherwise.

Having spent twenty-eight years in the ring, boxing, of course, was an important and interesting part of my life, and later in this book I will tell all about it—both the good and the bad. But first I want to tell you about another part of my life, a part far removed from prizefighting, yet strangely close to it.

As a teen-ager I had been caught stealing seven dollars from a streetcar and was sentenced to three years in a Missouri reform school. I had been assigned to the brickyard, which was tough duty. However, I had broken my hand in a fight and was transferred to the laundry, where the work was lighter, but the heat and humidity were almost unbearable. It was then that I made up my mind. There were two ways to go, you understand, and only two. Either I could continue stealing, in which case I knew that I would eventually be caught and sent back to reform school—or prison when I was older; or I could start to climb my first glass mountain and try to get out of

the ghetto by pursuit of an honest living. I decided that I
wanted no more of reform schools.

But what to do? This was the next thing I had to make
up my mind about. I felt that resuming a formal education was out, but I wanted to achieve fame and fortune in
some endeavor to make up to my aunt and mother the
shame I had brought on them, especially after the great
effort they had made to insure that I would be a good,
honest man.

I wanted to prove that they were right and that their
training had not been a waste, and I wanted to make
something of myself. I liked baseball, but ruled that out
because at that time blacks were making no progress in
that field. The only black baseball player who was doing
anything at all in those days was the great Satchel Paige.
On the other hand, you see, black fighters were doing
well: some main-eventers were getting close to $1,000,
which was a lot of money in those days. I felt that a musical career would take too long and was too uncertain, and
even though I loved music I didn't feel that I could
achieve my goal.

I loved to box, so, after taking everything into consideration, I decided that boxing would be my bag. I made up
my mind that I was going to be the best in the business
by learning everything I could and training hard to perfect my ability and physical condition. I wasn't quite sixteen years old when I made this decision, and had seen
only one professional fight—one in which Benny Deathpane, a well-known fighter at that time, had participated.
I was impressed by the excitement and the action, and I
felt that I could develop the skill and physical fitness to
become a good fighter. I knew I had the guts, the desire
and the motivation—and I wanted the money.

As a member of the Junior Mason's drill team, I had

learned discipline, so the rigid discipline of the reform
school was not as tough a problem to me as it was to most
guys, and I was thankful for that, for the punishment was
pretty rough. The two worst offenses in the eyes of the
officials were attempted escapes and sex offenses, and
boys who had been caught were beaten with a leather
belt that was four inches wide and a quarter of an inch
thick. The belt was attached to a wooden handle and was
applied so vigorously that the pants of the offender would
stick to his backside with blood. I never received the belt
treatment, but I once received a switching. This didn't
bother me too much, as I used a ring technique of crowding an opponent. By crowding the switch the man wield-
ing it couldn't get full leverage.

I boxed while in reform school and in my first year
scored sixteen knockouts, which gave me a reputation the
other boys respected, so they never picked on me, and
this kept me out of a lot of trouble, you see. Boxing was
also a great outlet for my youthful energies and emotions.
I was fortunate at this time to receive a considerable
amount of help with my boxing from Eddie Jones, who
was three years older than me and had quite a bit of experience in the ring.

It's funny how you don't miss something until it's taken
away from you. While I was in reform school I used to
dream of how nice it would be just to get an affectionate
pat on the head or a kiss from a loving mother or aunt.
And to taste home cooking again! I would drool at the
thought of it. I thought that I would even enjoy a spank-
ing from a loved one, as it would be administered with
love, and love was one thing that there was certainly
none of in reform school.

There was plenty of stealing still going on in the
"school." The kids stole from each other and from the

guards, and the only reason some of them smoked was because the other boys would know they had stolen from a guard, as they were the only ones who were allowed cigarettes, so respect for the smoker soared. Blacks were separated from the whites, but all were treated equally and a spirit of comradeship and democracy prevailed among the inmates, which often happens among people who share the same problems.

It was while in reform school that I first began to formulate my Any Boy Can program. I wanted to keep boys from going wrong and winding up in reform school. It wasn't a pleasant experience: the confinement, every move being watched, having to obey every whim of the guards. And there always were some guards who delighted in being sadistic and brutal, possibly to satisfy their ego and prove to themselves that they had authority and power. Even worse than the beatings, the hard work and the poor living conditions was the loss of dignity and freedom—the feeling that one is a caged animal. Most of us take our freedom to come and go as we please for granted, and do not appreciate this freedom until it is taken away.

I was paroled after twenty-two months and made a vow that I would never again do anything that would cause me to be sent back to reform school or jail. I have kept that vow. In 1960 I did go back to the Missouri reform school, but I went back as a world-champion boxer to talk to the boys.

"I was an inmate here," I told them. "But I want to assure you that this is not the end, but the beginning for you. I know it was for me. It was my crossroad. I made up my mind that they would never have any reason to get me back, and I also made up my mind that when the opportunity arose I would do my best to help keep every boy I could to stay out of this institution and places like it.

"I'm here to help you. God helped me to accept the things I couldn't change, the courage to change the things I could change that needed changing and the wisdom to know the difference. And He will do the same for any and all of you if you'll give Him the chance."

I was always well-received in penal institutions because they knew the advice I gave them was good, because I had been down that road myself. In a talk at the Indiana reformatory, I said, "I am used to coming to places like this. I was an inmate once myself. I'm not trying to preach to you. We all make mistakes. I made one and spent twenty-two months in a Missouri reform school as a result. I know what goes on inside reform schools, and I know from firsthand experience what goes on inside an inmate's mind. So let me assure you that you boys and young men are still young enough to change your lives. You have great chances to get out of here and lead good, productive lives and make something worthwhile out of yourselves. Just choose the right road and follow it. You can do it!"

While I was still boxing, I didn't have the time to really get going with my youth programs, but I took every opportunity I had to speak to underprivileged youngsters and help them whenever I could. I remember speaking to a group in Portland, Oregon, and I revealed to them how a little poem given to me by my auntie, Willie Pearl Moore, was responsible for much of my success in and out of the ring.

She had told me, "When a task is once begun, never leave it until it's done. And if the labor is great or small, do it well or not at all." This was beautiful, outstanding.

I told the children, "That little poem has kept me

going for years. When I got knocked down, inside or outside the ring, that's what made me get up. That's why I'm
teaching youngsters today that they all have something
worthwhile to offer the world if they try hard enough.
Never give up. I'm not trying to teach black power or
white power. I'm trying to teach youth power and brain
power. That's the kind of power that will make you better and happier adults. You've got to learn moral and
spiritual values, and then you won't be a juvenile or an
adult delinquent. You'll get somewhere in life, and on the
way you'll pick up a lot of joy and satisfaction. You won't
get anywhere being bitter and feeling sorry for yourself.
You just keep believing you've got what it takes and keep
punching away, and you'll come out a winner."

I always enjoyed talking to youngsters and took every
opportunity to do so. I felt that if I kept even one kid
from becoming a delinquent, it was worthwhile. And
these talks were helping, you understand. I got a lot of
personal satisfaction out of them. I was learning how to
get to young people—all of which fitted in with my
bigger plans to help youth when I retired from boxing.
The pieces were beginning to fall into place.

THREE

•

I know that people are still interested in my ring career, as they are always asking me about my different fights. Granted, it was an exciting, formative, educational and satisfying time of my life, and as I promised, I will tell all about it later in this book, but first I would like to talk about now, as this is important to all of you, you understand.

Helping youth, and particularly disadvantaged youth, is really my bag, but along the way I found that there were many other areas that are in great need of help, such as civil rights, poverty, juvenile delinquency, drug abuse, student unrest and crime in the streets. I do what I can to help correct these problems, but my main thing is helping youth, because this is where it all begins; this is the root of the whole thing. If we can get our youngsters going up the right path, then many of these other problems will be solved automatically. Young boys and girls will know that all people are created equal regardless of color or religion, and entitled to equal rights, and it will be a natural thing for them to accept this fact. And proper education will prepare our youth so that they can take advantage of the opportunities that exist in America, and they will be happy, prosperous people, and when you have happy, prosperous people who are getting their fair share of the good things we have here, you know, you have people who are satisfied and want to keep our form of government instead of wanting to overthrow it. And poverty, juvenile delinquency, unrest and crime will decline greatly. I'm not trying to say that these things will be eliminated completely, but they will be reduced to the point where they can be easily controlled.

I plunged into youth work after leaving the ring, all bright-eyed and bushy-tailed and eager to prove that my program would work. But I found that, just as always in my life, my goals would not come easily. With my head in the clouds, I forgot that very down-to-earth fact that when you get down to the nitty-gritty, the plans I had in mind needed money, and lots of it.

People would listen to my ideas and tell me how great they were, but that's about all I'd get from them—lip service. It was quite a while before people started putting their money where their mouth was. In the meanwhile it cost me many thousands of dollars of my own hard-earned money. But I'm not kicking, because it was money well spent, and the rewards were great.

After leaving the ring I worked in movies and television for a while, appearing in "Huckleberry Finn," "The Carpetbaggers," "Fortune Cookie," "Wagon Train," "Perry Mason" and several others; but all the while I was developing my Any Boy Can program. I also worked part-time for the Office of Economic Opportunity as a job-corps consultant.

Meanwhile, I wanted to test ABC and determine how well it worked with different age groups, so I taught the concept to my boy Hardy; my adopted son Billy Daniels; Nua Moa, a Samoan; and Ed B. Rivers' grandson Donnie. The ages of these boys ranged from four to twenty-two years, so I had a good cross-section to work with. I put them through the ritual I had developed, which was carried out in a somewhat military fashion because all boys like to play at being a soldier, and because discipline leads to self-discipline, which is an important ingredient for success, you understand. I taught them self-defense and how to box professionally, and it worked for all of them, so I knew it would work for all ages on a larger scale—at least nationally, and possibly internationally. This pilot program made these boys grow almost immediately, and I was quite happy to see the wonderful changes in them after just a short time.

On an impulse, I took Billy to Los Angeles and he boxed three rounds against an experienced fighter, and he looked like a pro—he was that good, and here it was the first time he had fought in the ring. Everybody was amazed, and I had offers for him to fight all over the country, and here he was only a novice amateur. He was a middleweight then, and only fifteen years old, so I kept him out of professional fighting until he had a chance to go to school and then make up his mind what he wanted to do. He is now a full heavyweight and is twenty years old, six feet tall and weighs 200 pounds. He is going to college now, majoring in physical education, and plays football, runs track and boxes. He's good at all these sports, and after he finishes college he may box professionally or play pro football for a while before settling down as an athletic director or coach. The ABC has done a lot for Billy, as, among other things, it has taught him to think for himself, and think positively.

Shortly after completing this experimental pilot program, I was invited to Jamaica and sponsored by the Jamaican Boxing Board of Control to train boys for the Olympics. In all I trained about six hundred boys, using

my ABC methods, and I enjoyed this immensely, as these
Jamaicans are beautiful people. This also gave me more
experience in developing my program and supplied further proof that it would work. I was working hard, but
enjoyed every minute of it. I had to accomplish in two
months what really should have taken six months, so I
had to work about fourteen hours a day, but it was worth
it.

It was in Jamaica that I met Carl Moxie, who was then
a welterweight, and a great one. He later became a middleweight, and he stayed with me in San Diego while he
went to school and boxed. He had plenty of class and
would have ranked with the best, but he was more interested in the computer field. Well, this is great. A man
should do his thing. He had to go back to Jamaica because of visa problems, and I most surely do miss that
pleasant young man. I was recently invited to return to
Jamaica, and I would like to again work with these beautiful people, but I am so tied up with my Boy Scout and
Any Boy Can work here that I don't think I will be able
to make it.

My big chance to get going with ABC and really prove
its worth in a way people can understand came in Vallejo,
California. A new development called Country Club
Crest was having a big vandalism problem and as a result
many of their units went unrented. The vandalism
amounted to something like $7,500 a month, and they
called on me and asked if I thought I could help them get
rid of this problem. I told them that I could help them
with my ABC program, so they put me on a salary and
told me to go ahead.

It turned out to be a lot tougher project than I thought
it would be, and there were times when I was frustrated,
disappointed and disgusted; and I almost gave up on it. I

put in long hours, and many times I had to dip into my own pocket for funds. In fact, I spent my entire salary plus thousands of dollars of my savings to keep going. For a while it just seemed like I wasn't getting anywhere, but I never tipped my mitt and let anybody know I was having problems. It's the same in the ring. You can't let a guy know when he hurts you or you're in big trouble. But I had confidence in my program and kept at it. I knew it would work.

I started out in Vallejo by setting up a punching bag in my yard, and while I was working the bag a young boy came up and watched for a while, then he said, "I bet I can do that." So I told him I thought he could too and that he should come back the next day with some of his friends and I'd give them all a crack at it. The next day the boy was back with about thirty of his friends and I taught them how to punch the bag and the fundamentals of boxing. I think almost every boy wants to know how to defend himself physically, because then he feels secure and important and doesn't have to take a lot of bull from anybody. This was the lure that attracted them to ABC. Then, when I felt I had them interested, I worked in moral and spiritual values.

But you can't win them all, you know, no matter how hard you try. I remember one boy who refused to join, so I asked him why. "What for?" he said. "To wear one of those stupid little caps and listen to you spout off about the Bible?" I told him I just wanted to make a man out of him. He said he already was a man and turned his back and walked away.

And there was the time when some boys set fire to our headquarters; and another time when they ransacked my office and broke all the windows, but gradually, with persistence and the help of the boys who had joined ABC,

many of the outsiders joined up, and the very few who
didn't join were afraid to try anything because they were
so few and realized that the well-trained and loyal ABC
boys would give them what for if they tried anything
funny. So Any Boy Can, after only a few months, was an
outstanding success in Vallejo. Vandalism dropped from
$7,500 a month to $5 or $10 a month at the most, and
since ABC was established only one of our Vallejo members has set foot inside juvenile hall in five years. And in
the San Diego ABC, only three members out of four hundred have been in trouble in the last three years. This is
beautiful.

The same thing can be accomplished anywhere, and I
won't be satisfied until ABC is established nationwide. It
won't be easy, you understand, but then anything worthwhile never is. And when ABC is nationwide, many of
our country's problems will be solved, for these boys and
girls are the men and women of the future—the men and
women who will guide our nation's destiny—and it is
vital that they learn proper moral and spiritual values
early in life. Sure it will be hard work and cost money,
but just imagine, if you will, the chain reaction resulting
from changing a juvenile delinquent into a respectable,
productive, law-abiding citizen. The thought is staggering
when you really think about it. You take a boy who could
wind up as a thief or murderer and make a man out of
him who might reach great heights. He could become a
scientist who might discover cures for incurable diseases.
He could become a great statesman—perhaps even be
elected President of the United States. The prospects are
unlimited when we bring out the latent talents in our
youngsters, but they need help along the way, and that's
where the Any Boy Can program, the Boy Scouts of

America and many other beautiful youth programs come on the scene.

The Vallejo experience was great in itself because of what it did for the boys, but I also had some experiences there that enriched my own life. I heard Pastor Byron Spears at a prayer meeting, and he completely captivated me and drew out things that had been difficult for me to understand. He preached that people should obey God's law—the Commandments—and he so impressed me that I found myself a candidate for baptism. After I was baptized, Pastor Spears suggested that I put God in the concept I was teaching the boys and teach them the Commandments. I told him that I thought this was a lot for these youngsters to learn, but he told me that as their leader I could put this in their minds, as they have a retention that is fantastic. So I started teaching them and offered a reward to the first boy to learn, and within a week one boy made it pretty good. Then another boy learned and challenged the first boy, and before long they all could do it. We learned by repetition and making a game or contest out of it, and pretty soon I found that I too had learned it. And when I learned the Commandments I found myself with my conscience really alive and sitting on my shoulder—riding right on my shoulder like a bird. Every time an evil or wrong thought would come into my head my conscience would say so, and the bad thoughts would be driven out of my mind.

I did not force the boys to take religion, you understand, but I encouraged them to pick up guidelines from the Scriptures, as I think these are the greatest guidelines in the world. And if these are not the greatest guidelines in the world, let somebody tell me what are and let them prove it to me, because otherwise I've wasted my life.

I had another experience in Vallejo that I will remember as long as I live, as it was one of the greatest things that can happen to a man. First of all, let me explain that the ABC concept was something that I picked up through life. I heard a bit here and a bit there, you see, and I put it together, and after I put it together in my memory— having a fantastic memory when I was young—I thought I could remember all these things. I had made the change from Baptist to Seventh-Day Adventist, and I was living clean, cleaner than I had ever lived in my life, because I wanted to be right. I wanted to do things right. I was in daily communion with the Holy Spirit. I felt that there was something missing from the ABC concept, and I was asking, beseeching and begging the Lord to give me something to help these young boys grow because I wanted to grow right along with them. One night I decided that I'd go to bed early, and as I was lying in bed I heard a knocking sound. There were four knocks—on the wall. Well, I sat up in bed. Then all of a sudden I said, "Face. Face what?" It seemed like this was the message coming through to me. Then I thought that maybe I was just imagining it, that perhaps I was overly tired, so I tucked myself under the covers once again, but as I did I heard the four knocks on the wall once again, this time clearer and more insistent than before. I sat up in bed again and said, "Face," because this is exactly what the knock said. "Face what? I'm in the room by myself. I have four bedrooms, but there is nobody in the house but myself. My wife and children are 500 miles away in San Diego, and I'm here in Vallejo, in Country Club Crest. Face what?" Then I got hold of my thinking and remembered. Anybody who has ever studied music remembers that notes between the lines on a musical score are called

F-A-C-E. Five lines that spell out E-G-B-D-F, and four spaces that spell F-A-C-E. I was looking for something basic, and here it was. *Face the future in harmony.* With who? *With all mankind.* Then I took E-G-B-D-F: Every Good Boy Does Fine. Then I counted to see if I could get five faces: white, black, red, yellow, brown. There are no more. *Those are the five faces of man. That means everybody.* This is beautiful, I thought. How sweet it is. Outstanding. God had answered my prayers, and I had my message. Face the future in harmony with all mankind. Then I went back to sleep, and I slept better that night than in—well, I don't know when. I really slept. And when I woke up the next morning I said, "Face. Face the future in harmony with all mankind. *All* mankind. E-G-B-D-F. Every Good Boy Does Fine, and every good boy deserves friends." It came out without even thinking. Then I went to work on it—I really went to work on it. I began to really put it all together, and out of this came the ABC concept. I go ahead with ABC the way I feel that God wants me to because I know that religion plays a great part in all our lives.

In 1967 I also organized the San Diego Any Boy Can club. We located this center right in the inner-city neighborhood, where it was needed, because I knew that these boys from low-income families could not afford to travel to get to the center. The program must be brought to the boys if it is to be effective. If you have something like ABC that boys want badly enough and you know how to administer it, you know, it will seem like a prize or reward for them to get into ABC. And it is, but you can't expect the impossible—like some kids without a cent getting to a center that is ten miles away from their home. That's why I say that the program has to be brought to the boys. They can't afford it any other way. I know it's hard for a lot of people to visualize anybody being that poor—but believe me, it's true.

The San Diego ABC received great acceptance and has grown to the point where we are going to move from the little store we now occupy to our own building, which will soon be built. Louis Lake is the director of the San Diego ABC and has been a great help to me. He is a graduate of San Diego State College, where he played on the varsity basketball team and graduated with a bachelor of science degree in psychology. He is an ex-marine and uses the knowledge gained in school and in the Marine Corps to control, guide and educate the boys. He is a sincerely dedicated man, a fine young man and a great example for the boys to follow. He is strict when there is need to be strict, but the boys know he is their friend and love and respect him.

In 1966 and 1967 I continued with my ABC work and combined this with lecture tours all over the country. In 1968 I was hired by the Boy Scouts of America and since that time have traveled over 200,000 miles for them. They are becoming aware of what ABC can do for scouting, and I hope we can work as a unit. Together we can do a great service for America and our youth.

I love the work I am doing, but I wish I didn't have to travel so much, as I miss my family. Being away puts so much responsibility for raising our large family on my wife, Joan, who is a wonderful person, a good mother and a good administrator. She's my right arm.

FOUR

•

I like to talk to youngsters every chance I get and try to encourage them, especially inner-city—or so-called ghetto—children, because they need this encouragement more than the others, you see. We must make these young black brothers and sisters feel important. Otherwise they will face tasks that seem to be insurmountable. And they won't feel important enough to even *want* to accomplish anything or be anybody, or *do* something more than the person lying around the avenue, drinking wine, wasting a life, the old men defeated early in their youth, now sitting around talking about their welfare checks they've got coming in, pensions and so forth.

So we want young people to go out and try. We want them to be aggressive enough to be progressive, come along with skills and valuable ideas of their own, to be able to hope and dream, reach out, then really do the things that are necessary in life to make an honest living, an honorable living, to really do proud to the whole human being, the whole human race, the total human race—not having to be called upon as one special group to have special legislation serve upon them to ensure them of rights that are already theirs, you see, and this is where a lot of our country's hang-ups are, because people are passing special rights such as civil rights. But we're talking about human rights in this area. We should talk about human rights—the rights that a human has: the right to life, liberty and the pursuit of happiness. And again you get a hang-up there—pursuit of happiness. No legislation nor no one can guarantee you, me or any other person happiness. But since the Declaration of Independence proclaimed this to be available to all of the people in the United States of America, why is it that it is cut off in so many areas, such as—and I'm going back a bit to my day and time—there were no blacks here, no blacks there, restaurants for white only, and all of this sort of carrying on, you see. That's a hang-up. So it went on in school systems and what-not. I remember in my day there was a young man back around 1932 who tried to go to a university in Missouri, St. Louis University, and he was denied that because he was black, so he filed a suit. I forget the name of the suit, but it can be found in the records in St. Louis.

Why should a man have to file suit for something that is his—that other people take for granted? That's why I say there should be no special legislation passed for me, because I'm an American as much as anybody in America is, and I don't ask for anything more than anybody else— nothing special. Just give me what the other citizens get, you see. And this is a hang-up. And so, that being the hang-up, you've got a lot of people fooled that they need special acts to insure them that they can live in certain places, but no special acts are needed, because all citizens are entitled to life, liberty and the pursuit of happiness. That encompasses many, many things and many, many fields, and many, many areas: housing, schooling, jobs and opportunities.

So this is where people are really hung up. I think that

out of all the pieces of legislation and all the pieces of literature that were read and declared, that the pledge of allegiance to the flag of the United States of America and to the Republic for which it stands, *one* nation under God, *indivisible* with *liberty* and *justice* for *all*, means more than all these other things put together. This is a two-way agreement, with the citizen pledging his allegiance and America promising liberty and justice, for *all*, and once this becomes a reality—with liberty and justice for all—then you have no problems here.

The white man would rather have the black man feel that this is his problem. This is *not* the black man's problem. This is the white man's problem, and he should face it. Because why? The black man was in Africa. He was brought here in bondage and chains, a slave, and he was forced to accept the white man's orders, his language and his religion—and his sins. He played a major part in building the country with labor.

There's a great scream about militancy. But who were the first militants? The white man, the New Englanders who threw the tea overboard because they didn't want to pay the tax on the tea to the British. And the first man that fell from the volley that the British fired was a black man, and his name was Crispus Attucks, fighting in a white man's revolution to insure the safety of the white man. And yet, he couldn't get a cup of tea. But he felt that if he fought for this cause, one day he would get his freedom, and all his people would get their freedom, so we come on down the line. And then we learn through history that draft-dodging is not new, you know. It's under many guises, but it's not really new. Because why? There were many New Englanders who had vast holdings at this time, and who were farmers and businessmen, and who had slaves, and they sent them in their stead, you know, to keep from going to war themselves. And so there were many first-class Minutemen who were black, and some notable black Minutemen such as Peter Salem, who shot and killed Major John Pitcairn of the British army, and Peter Poore and Cuff Whitmore and many others who were first-class fighting men, because why? They were fighting for their lives. They were fighting for their freedom. Freedom meant everything to them, because a life doesn't mean anything unless a person is free. So they were fighting for more than just their lives. They were fighting for the freedom of the yet unborn blacks.

And so it went, and you read about where the civil war produced many great black fighters. The troops from Massachusetts came down and crossed over there into Charleston, South Carolina, and came out with honors. It took almost a hundred years after the Civil War for the white man to feel that the black man was a fighting man, because Lincoln didn't really want them to fight. Washington didn't want them to fight. But it took almost a hundred years for them to find out that the black man was a fighting man. But the black man has everything to fight for, because he has been deprived and kicked and booted around since way back.

And now the young people are saying, "If not now, when? If not here, where? If not you, who?" They're tired of waiting. And so you get hang-ups in the colleges because something's been kept from these youngsters and they want Negro history to be taught—or so-called *black* history, since it's fashionable now to use the word "black"—by black teachers. But some of the officials say that we can have black history, but it shall not be taught by black teachers. Well, who could better teach black history than black teachers? So another hang-up.

But we want to talk about something that's going to be

really positive and help all people start off together with their best foot forward. We'll talk about harmony. E-G-B-D-F—Every Good Boy Does Fine—black, white, red, yellow and brown. But they must work hard and live in harmony. That's your power. Youth power. See? The Boy Scouts of America will be happy to tell you that they believe in youth power. This is great, and I work for the Boy Scouts in the area of community relations. Why they call me a specialist, I don't know, because I feel that a specialist is a person that usually knows a lot about a little. Anyway, I have been doing remarkably well with the ABC program. I teach moral values, spiritual values and the physical value of self-defense. But I only teach basics. I feel that basics are enough to get the young person started. And this is not just for blacks, or just for whites, but applies to blacks, whites, reds, yellows and browns. The whole spectrum. This is the face of man. You get the whole ball of wax in one fist. That's where the power comes from.

I would like to help bring this about in a harmonious way. I'm trying to enlist young people who can help me, you understand. And who could help me better than a man who had somehow lost his way in life and then found himself again? Then he could be of help to some boy who missed out on the things that he missed out on when he was young.

And there is Instructor Louis Lake at the ABC center, and other people who show great interest in helping young boys. I have three young boys of my own, and certainly I want my boys to face the future in harmony with their fellow man and not be afraid of anything, because when one is afraid of something one fails to express himself.

I think it is also important to show our ghetto youth

how things can be available to them when they work for them. I think that discipline is a key to my program, self-discipline. And I feel that most of the boys in my program have made wonderful strides in changing their attitudes. When you change a young man's attitude, you've got him walking the right way.

But we need help so ABC can expand, and I think that this could be accomplished with, among other things, the aid and funding of private individuals and private industry, because private industry is involved, you understand. For example, a man who owns a supermarket and has a lot of children around the neighborhood who are committing vandalism, breaking windows, stealing and throwing fire bombs and what not, he is the one who will lose financially. But, if he is wise, he will get his neighboring businessmen together and organize an ABC program. Then he'll see the attitudes change in those youngsters. When a youngster is in ABC and works eight weeks and learns the ritual, he becomes a motivated person, a proud person, because he has learned something that his contemporaries walking the streets don't know. He feels that he can defend himself if anybody should try to bully him. He will not stand to be bullied. He will walk away from trouble if he is allowed to, but he will not be bullied.

And on the other hand, I may find a young man who has the latent ability to be a great fighter, and I will coordinate the whole thing and he will be that great champion he wants to be. Then he can help young children more than I could, because he will be of an age where he can relate to them easily. He would draw youngsters to him rather than run them away from him, and they would like to relate with him because he is a young man.

I also feel that if we could get government heads like Governor Ronald Reagan and President Nixon involved in ABC, it would help. I have talked to many of these people, and they are interested, as they recognize the tremendous potential ABC has to help the nation. They are solidly behind us, and I hope we will receive material help from them soon. Of course, the Boy Scouts have been on the scene for almost sixty years, and it is a beautiful organization, but ABC can work hand in hand with the Boy Scouts. One will help the other.

Now there is black pride, and I take great pride in trying to help develop and change attitudes of young boys. Here I am, my ring days over, gray and balding, teaching young boys, doing what I can to fight juvenile delinquency, doing what I can to make this a better America for all of us. And when one of my boys makes it big I'm proud of him. I'm happy to have been given the opportunity to help. Happy to help him avoid the misfortunes I had. Then this boy will go on to teach other young boys moral, spiritual and physical values that Archie Moore taught him, and then these boys that he taught will go on to teach still others the things they were taught, and they in turn will teach others. This is what I am proudest of. This is beautiful.

FIVE

●

Our present ABC center is a storefront located in the inner city. The center is divided into two sections. In front are two desks placed off to one side, and in the middle of the room are two Ping-Pong tables and three small billiard tables. In the back room, which is completely separated by a wall, is a boxing ring, a heavy bag, a speed bag and other boxing equipment.

"Good afternoon, students," I say when they enter.

The students look up at me and with a firm handshake say, "Good afternoon, Instructor Moore." Once a student failed to look at me and spoke in a rather timid way. "No, no, no!" I warned. "Look me right in the eye when you speak, and let's hear it loud and clear!"

The student again extended his hand. This time his handshake was firm, and he looked me right in the eye, and his voice was strong.

"That's better," I complimented him. "Always look a man right in the eye and speak with confidence."

I am justly proud of these boys. They are a neat, clean, well-mannered group of youngsters, although for the most part their clothes are old and somewhat ragged. The atmosphere is formal, except when the boys are playing, and then, of course, they make as much noise as other youngsters. But there is a distinct show of respect between students and teachers. The students are always addressed as *Student* before their name, and they address me as *Instructor Moore*.

One day we went to the gym section where Billy Daniels was taping his hands. He wore a pair of new blue trunks I had just bought him, with a red top and red shoes.

"All right, Billy," I said when he finished taping his hands, "let's get to work on that jab." I stood facing Billy and held my open palm toward him. "Now," I said, "I'm going to say the word 'out,' but I'm going to pronounce it as if it had two syllables. I'll say 'ow-tuh,' and when I say the 'ow,' you jab, but by the time I say 'tuh' I want you back in your original starting position. Okay?"

"Okay," Billy replied, and he assumed his stance.

"Ow-tuh!" I barked, and Billy's left fist snapped out and struck my palm with a sharp, slapping sound, then snapped back to its original position. It wasn't too bad, but I wasn't satisfied. "No, no, no," I said. "You're too slow on the recoil. You do that against a good man and the next thing you know you'll wake up in the dressing room. Let's try it again."

I held my palm up again, and Billy took his stance. "Ow-tuh! Ow-tuh! Ow-tuh!" I repeated time and again. And Billy's fist snapped out and back, each time a little faster, until finally I was satisfied. "Good," I said. "Work on the bag for a while, then I'll get someone to spar a few rounds with you." I turned to the group of ABC members who had been watching. "Now," I told them, "let's do the concept."

The boys quickly lined up in front of the heavy bag. "We teach boys how to walk away from trouble," I told them. "We teach them what it means to have dignity.

Dignity is a thing that you earn. Respect is a thing that
you earn. Respect should be a mutual thing—a two-way
street. If you respect me, well, you know I'm going to respect you, because you know that I have common intelligence, and I feel that you have common intelligence
enough to respect your friends, your fellow man, your
neighbors, or anybody. So, in other words, you breed a
mutual respect. Now, I don't say—the Bible says—'Love
ye one another.' Christ says it, but I can't say it. I'm not
Christ. But I say if you respect me and I respect you, that
opens the door and gives love a chance to come in. Do
you understand?"

"Yes, sir," the boys responded.

"You remember when all of you first came here, looking down, wouldn't look at me. Now you look at me.
You're a student. You're identified, and you respect me
and I respect you. What do you call me?"

"Instructor Moore," they responded.

"Instructor Moore. That's right. Because I respect all
of you. You know I respect you. I take you with me. I
give you the best of everything I can. I see that other people give you the best of everything they can when I'm involved in something with you. You travel a lot. How
many functions have you been to, Student Monia?"

"At least eighty," the boy replied.

I've taken them to many places, and they see how people on the other side of the tracks live. They see how they
eat, and how they have fun, and how they have nice
things, and this is the thing that makes them want to be
something, to be somebody, to do something, so that they
can have the better things in life.

"In order to do something," I told the boys, "you have
to do it in an orderly manner, and the first thing is to
achieve discipline, self-discipline. And when you achieve

self-discipline you can form your organization. Then you can function. But when you're unruly, and everybody's trying to talk, and everybody's trying to be the leader, nothing happens, but when one man in this group can lead you, you're really on the ball." Then I suggested that one of the boys lead the program that evening and indicated him.

The boy went to the end of the line, stepped out about a foot in front, turned so that his left side was facing the group and his right side facing me. Thus by turning his head he could address either the boys or me.

"All right," I said, "now talk in a loud and clear voice."

"Good evening, students," the boy began.

"Good evening, Instructor Randall," the students replied in unison.

"Say good evening to Instructor Moore."

"Good evening, Instructor Moore."

"And the new students."

"Good evening, new students."

"We will now salute the flag. Attention!"

The boys snapped to attention with military precision.

"Salute!" the leader ordered.

"I pledge allegiance to the flag of the United States and to the Republic for which it stands, *one* nation under God, *indivisible*, with *liberty* and *justice* for *all*."

The leader ordered, "As you were." The boys then assumed an at-ease position.

"We are on a brand-new concept in teaching," the leader said. "And what is this concept?"

"It is the ABC concept of moral, spiritual and physical self-defense for young people," the boys chorused.

"And what does this ABC mean?"

"Any Boy Can, if he wants to."

"If he wants to what?"

"Improve myself in all good things I do in order to become a better student in school and a better American."

"We are on a certain letter in teaching. What is this letter?"

"A."

"How do you know it to be an A?"

"Because you gave it to me."

"I gave it to you. How?"

"In a mysterious manner."

The leader indicated two of the students. "Step forward with your best foot and explain what this triangle means." He held his two hands in front of him, thumbs touching to form the base, and forefingers touching to form the sides.

"This is an A, or triangle, made up of three parts," the students replied. "The bottom part is the balance, or foundation. One side is correct delivery and recoil. Part of the other side is step in, jab and drag. The remaining portion is still quite a mystery."

"Thank you. Step back." He indicated two other students. "Step forward," he ordered, "and explain what this A, or triangle, can hold."

"This A, or triangle, can hold as much as you place upon it, as long as it is the truth, for the rest of your life."

"Thank you. Step back." Then to the group, "Attention!"

The students hastened to comply.

"What is the first thing that is taught in this class?" the leader asked.

"Good sportsmanship at all times," came the reply.

"Good sportsmanship can mean many things. But first it means—"

"You play fair and square at all times."

"And if you play fair and square at all times, then you are clean—"

"Inside and outside."

"If a student is clean inside and outside at all times then he must be—"

"A good student."

"Very well, good students, adjust your thinking caps and think of what a good student would not do. Would not do."

One by one the students rapidly called out the answers without hesitation: "Lie—cheat—steal—smoke—drink—gamble—refuse to go to church—refuse to go to school—commit vandalism—be in riots—sniff glue—break doors down—peddle narcotics of any kind—play with needles—break into empty houses—be a juvenile delinquent—push little kids into swimming pools—burn schools down—throw rocks at passing cars—set forest fires—set canyons on fire—tear Scriptures out of the Bible—cuss your mother—cuss your preacher—"

"Very well, good students," the leader broke in. "Adjust your thinking caps once more. This time we will think what a good student would do, could do, or should try to do in order to become that better student in school and that better American."

Once again the answers came rapidly and clearly: "Go to church—be a good American—go to school—get a high school diploma—become a lawyer—a doctor—preacher—teacher—evangelist—architect—store manager—instructor at the ABC club—lab technician—contractor—paleontologist—gas-station manager—gas-station owner—shoe man—go into politics—go into athletics—be a baseball player—football player—boxer—play hockey—handball—run track—play jai alai—race mo-

torcycles—be an all-around sportsman—boat racer—
jockey—sky diver—swimmer—be a fireman—fire chief—
be a policeman—police chief—judge—mayor—serve
your country—FBI—senator—secretary of state—detec-
tive—congressman—CIA—secretary of defense—vice
president—President—"

"Well, you can't go much higher than that," the leader
cut in.

"Very good," I said. "This is beautiful."

"What do the moral precepts mean?" The leader asked
the group.

"It is the good that is inside a person."

"Sometimes we must protect these moral precepts
through the physical—"

"Concept."

"How would you step off in life?"

"With my best foot forward."

"Upon which word?"

" 'Position.' "

" 'Position' is a simple word. It has how many syllables?"

"Three."

"Upon the last syllable, which is—"

"*Shun.*"

"Upon the last syllable you will find yourself in the correct boxing position, or fighting stance, ready, willing and
able to protect your moral precepts, which were laid
down especially for you. Po–si–*shun!*" he commanded.

The students obeyed, the right-handed youths with
their left foot and arm forward and their right fist cocked
at shoulder level, while the left-handed students assumed
the position in reverse.

"Upon the command 'out,' you will extend your fist
and extend it only. Ready—out!"

The little fists shot out in the motion of a boxer making a jab.

"Students," the leader asked, "why do you extend your fists in such a manner?"

"It is the correct way in order to hurt your opponent but not your fist."

"Recoil!"

The little fists snapped back to their original positions.

"Students, why do you recoil your fists back into the upright position?"

"It is the correct way in order to strike again like a cobra or an automatic."

The leader had the students go through the jabbing and recoiling motion several times, then he said, "This time we will convert this movement into one quick sequence making it a complete jab, so swift that Instructor Moore can hardly see it. Between the two syllables *ow* and *tuh*, your hand must be back into the upright position, so it has to be fast. Ready—ow-tuh, ow-tuh, ow-tuh."

He repeated the command many times, and each time the students complied with a speedy jab and recoil. When he was satisfied, he said, "As you were. This time we will do the step in, jab and drag. Po–si–*shun!*"

The students assumed their fighting stances.

"Ow-tuh!"

The fists shot out once again as their front feet stepped in against an imaginary opponent.

"Drag!"

The fists and feet returned to their original position. This movement was done several times until the leader was again satisfied. "As you were." he said finally. "How," he asked, "does a good student walk away from trouble?"

"Without cowardice, but with courage and dignity."

"But why does that good student walk away from trouble?"

"Because I learn the moral, spiritual and physical self-defense for young people."

"Very good. Now explain the flowers."

"All the flowers of all the tomorrows are in the seeds of today."

"Thank you. We will now all recite our famous four-line poem that we live by. Begin."

"When a task is once begun, never leave it until it's done. If the labor is great or small, do it well or not at all!"

"Thank you." The leader turned to me. "Any questions, Instructor Moore?"

"No, thank you," I replied.

"Class dismissed."

The boys broke their ranks and went about amusing themselves in various ways. Some went in front, where they played Ping-Pong or pool, another group gathered in a corner around a beat-up old set of drums and sang in rhythm as one of the boys beat the drums, a few others stayed to watch Billy train.

This is our method of group-teaching, of group-therapy, in self-defense from the mind angle, from the mental angle, from the heart angle, you see. Spiritual values and physical courage—all in one ball of wax. Walking away from trouble without cowardice, but with courage and dignity. And we intend to go much further. We want and are going to have instructors who are going to teach these youngsters how to play basketball, baseball and football. We need people who will come in and counsel these young people, teach them and help them catch up with their schoolwork.

We motivate these youngsters. When they do good work in school and around here, we reward them. We take them places, give them things. When we take them places, we show them how people live who have more than they have. We teach them not to be envious of these people but to work hard to improve themselves so that some day they and their children can have all these nice things. We teach them that it's up to them, that they can't have things handed to them on a silver platter— that they have to work to get them.

SIX

●

I was away from home for two weeks touring the country
on behalf of the Boy Scouts, and when I returned home I
learned that my wife had set up an appointment for me
with Lenny Pearl for the following morning. Lenny is a
writer with whom I had agreed to collaborate in writing
my life story. At first I treated him with just the same
courtesy and cooperation I gave all writers and had no
personal feelings toward him. But as time went on I
found that he respected me, my race and my religion, and
I in turn respected him, his race and religion, and out of
this mutual respect a great friendship developed. Lenny
soon became very interested in the Any Boy Can program and is now my assistant in this work.

Promptly at 8 A.M., Lenny showed up, so we went to
my den, where we could talk in privacy. The den is a
large room with a picture window facing the Wabash
Freeway, above and some distance away. In the center of
the den I have a pool table, as playing pool is one of my
favorite ways of relaxing. Off to the left there is a stair-
way leading to the upper floors, and off to the right, a few
steps higher than the den, is the living room, with a nice
fireplace and a piano that gets a lot of use. I'm proud of
my home, as it is something that I always dreamed of hav-

ing when I was a boxer and had no place I could really call home. It is located in the inner-city section of San Diego, and I keep it looking nice.

The walls of the den are covered from one end to the other with championship belts, trophies, plaques and framed newspaper stories pertaining to my ring career, and Lenny busily studied them while I read a letter that had arrived a few days earlier. When I finished, I motioned Lenny to a chair near the picture window and pulled up a chair opposite him. I held up the letter.

"I think this may be interesting to you," I said. "I had a press conference in San Francisco last week, and the reporter who conducted it sent me this letter and tape." I read the letter: "Your ABC program and the Boy Scouts seem ideally suited for one another, particularly on your little engine starting the big engine theory. I am enclosing the tape of our conversation because you expressed interest in hearing it. Please keep it with our compliments."

I placed the tape on my tape recorder and switched it on. The first few words were not distinguishable, but then it cleared up and I heard my voice: "Well," I was saying, "I work for the Boy Scouts of America, and the Any Boy Can is a group that I formed in Vallejo, California, in 1965. It was a tremendous vandalism and delinquency deterrent, and it proved to be of great value in the housing tract called Country Club Crest. They had 850 homes and 350 were vacant, and I asked why, and was told it was because vandalism was so rampant, and I told them I could fix this up easily.

"They asked me how, and I told them with ABC, a youth delinquency-deterrent program that would wipe out vandalism and crime. They told me to go ahead with it, so we installed ABC, and in three months time the vandalism dropped from a reported $7,500 a month to less than $70 a month, then as time went on it diminished until it finally got down to $5 or $10 a month at the worst."

"Why?" a reporter cut in. "Is it because you keep them busy at something else?"

"Yes. I was teaching them a basic youth-motivation program. Teaching them spiritual values, moral concepts and physical self-defense, but the way I taught it was in one ball of wax, through signs and symbols. This is something bordering on the mystique that all youngsters like. They like to know there's a place they can go and hide and come out with something better than the next person. They know more than their contemporaries in school because they know the ritual of the ABC concept, and knowing that, they felt proud and emboldened by the fact that they were learning self-defense. This being so, kids that used to pick on them began to take notice and stopped bothering them after receiving a couple of bloody noses, and ABC was really on its way. The ABC imbeds in the member's mind things that others take lightly. Take, for example, the Pledge of Allegiance. Most youngsters who go to school say it matter-of-factly, not really understanding what they are saying—only mouthing words. But the ABC boys are taught to understand what each and every word means—then they know what they want.

"They *know* that they are a part of this great American society, because it is deeply imbedded in their subconscious mind, then as they grow a little bit older they find out what they have been saying all this time they go for this thing that's called equality. They go to it in the right manner because the concept of the ABC is basic. It teaches them the things to strive for in life. Once this is imbedded in their minds they begin dreaming, and they have a lot of things to dream and pick from, because they know basically how to divide the right things from the wrong things. With this great concept in their minds and in their hearts, they stick with it."

"Is ABC tying in with the Boy Scouts?"

"Well, this is what we're talking about, and I suppose one of these days Boy Scouts will get around to it, because they have a tremendous drive on now for youngsters in the ghetto, and this is the way I can reach boys in the ghetto, and this is the way I have been reaching them. Maybe the Boy Scouts will come in soon. I hope they do, because it's a worthwhile thing. The Boy Scouts are a beautiful organization, and I hope that a lot of boys will join, because they have a lot to offer. Of course, my ABC program is a starter. It's like on a Caterpillar, you have a little starter engine that starts the big engine turning. Well, the Boy Scouts are the big engine, but they need a starter, and the ABC could be the starter."

"Don't you think, Archie, that outfits like the Black Panthers could follow your example? They've got a powerful organization. Why don't they turn it in the same direction?"

"This could be done. This could be done easily enough."

"Have you ever tried to talk to any of the Black Panther leaders?"

"Well, I have not come to know any of them well enough to discuss these matters with them. Perhaps if they would come to me I would be apt to talk with them, and we could do a great thing for youth."

"In other words, you do feel that they have a potential, because they are strong-minded men, and if they were pointed in the right direction they could be really great leaders. Do you feel that way, or am I wrong?"

"Let's not point directions for people, because people usually go in the direction they want to go. Whether they're right or wrong, it's not for me to decide. I'm not a judge. I'm not sitting in judgment. We could point the long bony finger at America as far as that is concerned. I'm saying that I'm out to help youth, regardless of the situation.

"So let's give these young people an opportunity. Let's give the Panthers an opportunity to prove that with this great organization they can do good things. Let's give everybody a chance. You see, being militant is not so bad in itself, because Webster defines "militants" as people who are ready to fight for a cause or an idea. And if the cause is just, it's worth fighting for. And I feel that the inequities to a lot of people give them a cause to fight for, and it's right to fight for a cause that brings about a social change, you know, that will give each boy what the Pledge of Allegiance says—let's put these words into action and make them working words—*liberty* and *justice* for *all*. And when you make that a working thing, then you've really got something going with all forces."

I switched the recorder off.

"Good interview," Lenny commented. "There's quite a bit in there that we can use."

I nodded. "That's why I played it," I said. "Now, where do we start?"

"Well, ABC is a great program," Lenny said, "and I know it's going to be a success. I think that strong emphasis in our book should be on what you are doing today and what you are planning to do in the future, but that we should also go into your past and tell about your early life and your ring career so that people can see just what you went through and how you came to be the way you

are now. I think your early life has been a strong in-
fluence in making you the way you are."

"Oh yes."

"Now, as far as the fighting goes—and you correct me
if I'm wrong—I felt that the two most important fights of
your boxing career were the first with Joey Maxim, in
which you won the world's championship, and the first
fight with Yvon Durelle in Canada, which I feel typifies
your character. In that fight you got off the canvas four
times before you finally knocked Durelle out. You just
wouldn't be beat. So what I would like you to do is go
over these two fights, blow-by-blow, your feelings mentally and physically, the crowd reaction, the reaction of
your handlers. Would you care to do that for me?"

"I'd be happy to," I replied. "I hope you don't run out
of tape."

"Nothing to worry about on that count," Lenny said.
"I've got about four hours worth left."

Well, I'll start with the Joey Maxim fight. But the Joey
Maxim fight doesn't start right with Joey Maxim. It starts
at the time I found myself in a very awkward situation,
hitting and missing, so to speak. Fighting in small towns
and getting little purses, and I felt that my talents were
much greater than the breaks I was getting, and I felt
that I would have to make a move if I was going to keep
on the timetable I had set in my mind—to start fighting
as a professional at the age of twenty-one and retire at
the age of twenty-seven and begin a family life. I thought
that this would really be good and that I could grow up
with my children, you see. I felt that I would have
enough money after winning the championship to afford
some of the things that a man would need, like a nice

home for my family and enough money to educate my
children properly, and to be able to help other young
people.

I had been fighting all over the country for thirty-five
dollars, ninety-five dollars, a hundred dollars. Eventually
I came to San Diego with a man named Felix Thurman, a
very fine person who had my interest at heart, but he
knew nothing about the fight game as such and soon sold
my contract to Jack Richardson for $250. Richardson car-
ried me to Australia, and I cleaned everybody's clock
over there and came back recognized as a title contender.
I then had a fight with Eddie Booker, who was also a top
contender. I think he was the middleweight champion of
California. We boxed to a ten-round draw, and I had to
knock him down three times to get that draw. This was
really severe competition.

The day after the Booker fight I became very ill and
was taken to the hospital, where they operated on me for
a perforated ulcer, and it was eleven long months before
I was able to fight again. And I couldn't have been able to
fight that soon if Felix Thurman hadn't come up with a
great idea as to how to protect the area where the doctors
had made the incision. He took a rubber foul cup, which
is the usual protection worn by a fighter, and slit the
heavy waistband, which extended quite high, and in this
slit he inserted an auto license plate, shaping it to fit the
contour of my abdominal area. He then sealed the slit
with a soldering iron, and I had great protection, both
physically and mentally. I also practiced very hard at
picking off left hooks to my body, as everybody in the
fight game knew about my operation and would be shooting for that weak spot. Maybe that sounds like dirty pool,
but it's all in the game and I couldn't really blame them.
In most sports you have to exploit your opponent's weak-

ness. In boxing, for example, I have seen fighters shoot jabs time and again for what they knew to be a weak spot over an opponent's eye, and once they had opened up a cut, continue until the fighter's efficiency became impaired because of the blood streaming into the eye, or, as in most cases, the fight would be stopped by the referee and a technical knockout awarded.

The same thing, to a certain extent, happens in football. A good quarterback is a marked man, and those big 250- to 300-pound defensive linemen do their best to get him. I don't think they are out to seriously injure him, but just jolt him hard enough to reduce his efficiency and confidence. And reversing the situation, a good quarterback is always trying to exploit the opposition's weakness, throwing or rushing against a rookie or a player who has been slowed by injuries, so you see, that's the name of the game. So, besides my armored license plate for protection, I trained hard to get into condition and to protect that right side my opponents would be shooting at. I trained like my life depended on it. That championship belt was something I *had* to win, and I wasn't going to let anything or anybody stand in my way. And besides, I was broke, dead broke, and badly in debt. I had to make some money. I got up early in the morning and did roadwork, then went to the gym and worked out on the speed bag and the heavy bag, jumped rope and sparred with anyone who was willing. I wore the armor-plated foul cup and found that it worked. Finally, I felt that I was ready and resumed my fighting career, winning my first five fights by knockouts.

I won four out of my next five fights, two by knockouts, and had one draw. Then I ran into a period where I just couldn't seem to get anywhere. I'd win a fight, lose a fight, just piddling around, and I told Richardson that I

didn't want to go any further with him. He told me I
could buy my contract for $450, but I didn't have the
money, so I got another man to buy it.

I decided that if I was going to fight anymore, it would
have to be in another part of the country, so I went with
Jimmy Johnston, the biggest promoter in the East, and his
brother Charley took over my management. This was in
1945, and from then on through 1951, I had 73 fights,
winning 62, losing 8 and drawing 3 times. Of my wins, 46
were knockouts, and I had fought the best in the country,
but still I had been unable to get a championship match
in all this time. It wasn't until 1951, while I was on a
South-American tour, that I received word that I was
matched to fight Joey Maxim for the title on December
17, 1952.

SEVEN

•

One day I met a man I had always wanted to meet—Jack Kearns. I had heard of him because he was a legendary figure in boxing and had been the manager of the great Jack Dempsey. It was a great day for me when he bought a piece of my contract. Kearns was a man who loved money, and I needed money. He always seemed to be able to get money from many sources, and he always seemed to have a lot of money. He had a knack of spending money, and he was a really big-timer in every sense. I liked Kearns because he believed in doing things in a big way, and I learned more from him in the few years that I was with him than I did in all the years I had been in the fight game. I really learned to like Kearns and respect him because he was fair to his fighter. He was for his fighter in every respect. I can say that about Kearns. I enjoyed a great career under Kearns and Charley Johnston, who were my co-managers.

But I got to dislike Johnston very bitterly because of his attitude toward people, especially minority people. Johnston showed me that when we went to Argentina. He had Sandy Saddler at the time, who was the featherweight champion, and he was giving all of his attention to Saddler. So when I asked him one day when I was going to have a championship, he almost bit my head off. Never did I want to strike a man so bad in my life as I did Johnston, but I knew that would ruin all my plans, you know, striking another guy in a foreign country. That would have been bad conduct and gotten me deported, and then I would probably never get a chance to fight for the championship, so I took these insults from Johnston. I still wanted the title, but I forbade him to come near me after a few fights. I didn't want him to come around me. I didn't care how he split the money with Kearns—I just didn't want to see Johnston's face, and this was the reason he wasn't in my corner when I fought Durelle.

The fight with Durelle I think was the absolute fight that every fighter hopes to have. This is the typical he-man fight that a fighter dreams about—getting knocked down and then being able to get up and conquer his opponent. Well, this is America, you see, and this is like the underdog coming through. America is the underdog, but it can rise to the occasion, I feel. But it has to rise to the occasion with all of the people working together. And when people work together, everybody must feel that they are an important cog of what it is that makes it work. This is where we are. So many people have been made to feel unimportant. Especially the black minority, the Mexican minority, the red minority—the Indian, you understand. He was the first man here. This was his country. He gets the worst rousting of anybody and suffers in silence. I feel deeply about those people, almost as much as I do about my own people. We helped build the country. We worked hard, broke our backs. We sweated, and we watched our women being taken advantage of, and we were afraid to speak out. Everybody wants to go to heaven, but everybody's afraid to die. Now the young people are going to be much bolder. They're going to de-

mand much more than I did. They're going to demand
their full and equal share. I'm going to teach them how to
demand their full and equal share, but I'm also going to
teach them *how to be qualified,* you understand. Social
change is inevitable. It has to be, you see, because this is
the name of the game. Everybody wants their freedom.
And these people are going to be willing to die for it.

You know, it's heartbreaking to see so many inequities.
This is a land of plenty, and yet so many people don't
have anything. Yet we spend billions of dollars on the
overseas program helping other poor people while our
minorities starve right here and live in ghettos and slums
with rats and roaches. And there are young people in
states like Mississippi who are dying on account of worms
being in their system due to lack of proper vitamins in
their food. And deficiencies cause their eyes to go bad
and cause so many other ailments, you understand.

We would like to get that thing they call equality. The
people who were back in the olden days, you understand,
they didn't like the oppression that was put on them.
They could only do so much about it. They did what they
could. You know, all the black man ever wanted—from
Frederick Douglass, an Abolitionist and runaway slave in
the 1800s, to Eldridge Cleaver—is equality. When you
get right down to it, equality makes some men what they
are, and inequality makes other men what they are.

And you see, there are people like Martin Luther King.
I feel that Mr. King was a beautiful leader. He wanted
things in a passive way, a nonviolent way, like Gandhi of
India. But things happen so fast that one demand brings
about another demand, you see, and when Martin Luther
King was shot off his balcony, he was fighting for the
rights of all people. *All* people, because he made this
statement loud and clear—that he wanted black children

and white children to enjoy what is in America. People in
Stone Mountain, Georgia, the Appalachians and all these
places, you see. The man was a great orator and a great
leader. And people who heard him believed him. But if
nothing happens, they get angry. Then you get angry
people. That's what I'm talking about. People say, "What
the heck, didn't Martin Luther King die for it? The white
man isn't going to give us the things that are already due
us. It's written in the Constitution and Declaration of Independence that *all* men are entitled to such as life, liberty and the pursuit of happiness." These people are tired
of waiting.

And you'll get some politicians who'll say, "Well this
was written for the white man." Well, let's rewrite it,
then. I mean, if it was written for the white man, let's
write something for the black man. Let's write the thing
over so it'll fit everybody. Of course, it really isn't necessary to rewrite the Constitution or the Declaration of Independence or the Pledge of Allegiance, because these
things were written for *all* men. But I'm saying that some
people would have you *believe* that it was written for
white people only.

I think it's common knowledge that the first man to die
in the Revolution was a black man (as I mentioned before, his name is Crispus Attucks), and perhaps he
couldn't get a cup of tea at a local establishment. And
you know what the bit was about. The British were trying
to impose tax on tea without representation, you see, and
this brought about a certain militancy among the whites.
Now, these men who fought a revolution for American
freedom were the first militants, and they had every right
to be militant, because they were being taken advantage
of. But if the word "militancy" is to be characterized by
the people from the inner city, it takes on a dark and un-

desirable connotation. Well, the militants, they didn't like the idea of paying tax for tea, did they? So they threw the stuff overboard, and that brought on the shots that killed Crispus Attucks. And that is why I define the word "militancy" every time I get a chance, because many people speak words without really knowing what they are talking about. Like they say "ghetto." This is a word that was used back in Biblical days when the Jews were in ghettos in Rome, and later in Russia. And then over here, in New York City, when the early people came in to settle, everybody lived in the ghetto together. Everybody lived together in the slum sections of the city, in the tenement flats, and everybody had their own little ghettos and things. But now the ghetto is associated with the blacks. People have a way of throwing words around with abandon, and sometimes they're meaningless and sometimes they're meaningful. I like to define these simple-sounding words that may have a lot of repercussions. When people find themselves defining these words and associating them with a certain people, it's often a gradual build-up into something that's foreboding and ominous.

You can go back and they will say that, well, Christianity is a white man's religion. Okay, granted it is. It's beautiful—if he would live it.

Back in the early days, as history will tell you, there were sixteen blacks who came over here before the early settlers, and they were free men. Then, later on, labor was needed to build a country, so the next blacks that came over here were bond servants, and they worked, and some of them got free, and some of them even owned white bond servants. But later on the slave traffic began, and slaves were such a popular thing—I mean for a man to own a slave, you know. To traffic in slaves was the greatest source of income there was. And the blacks over

here today are the offspring of the strongest of those who
were captured in Africa. You know why? Any man that
could survive the things they had to go through to get
here had to be strong. They had to sit down in the ship's
hold. They were chained hand-to-hand and foot-to-foot
and had to ride from the west coast of Africa to Jamaica
and then were separated from their families and sold. But
let me tell you how they rode. They rode in the shallow
subdeck of the ship. They couldn't stand. They had to sit.
They had to eliminate on the spot. They stank. They were
filthy. They had sores, and many of them died en route.
At least half of them died, because when a cargo ship left
Africa with three hundred slaves, it was lucky to have
one hundred and fifty alive when it got to Jamaica. And
as they died they would be cut loose from their chains
and be thrown overboard into the sea. I guess the sharks
followed the ships, you know.

The black man lived through that. He had to have
faith, faith in living and wanting to live. This is what happened to many people, and yet the white man must have
thought, well, this is a weak man because he captured
him in Africa and brought him here. But like I said, in
order to get here he had to survive the hardships that
only the strong could endure. I mean sitting down all that
time. There was no way for them to get up, and they had
to sit there in their own eliminations, and the flies and the
vermin, and it's no wonder half the people died.

Labor was the thing in those days, and everybody
wanted a slave, so this is what happened. Of course, only
the people who were affluent enough could afford slaves,
and a lot of shady things went on. And I would not rule it
out about how many mulattoes were offsprings of white
men and black women for the sake of having slaves. Well,

that's neither here nor there. It is a fact, I suppose. There are too many mulattoes for it to not be a fact.

So far a lot of people have not had the opportunity to pursue happiness. Until lately blacks couldn't even pursue an education. But this has changed greatly now. And this may be why more youngsters are seeking better education in colleges, and some of them demanding to be taught black history. And they can see where the black forefathers were not really the Uncle Toms that people said they were. They wanted things, and they had to go to all kinds of extremes to get these things. This is all documented, and I'm telling you these things so you can understand why there are so many angry people. Angry people who are tired of waiting.

But I started to tell you about the Durelle fight, so let's get back to that. The fight was about a minute old when he caught me with a right hand. I didn't see the right hand, but I felt it. It seemed like a bomb exploded in my head, and the first thing that struck the floor was the back of my head. And I felt a trickle of blood run inside my mouth, and I knew I had a concussion. And I thought, well, this is the way they happen. Concussions happen this way when you land and strike the back of your head on any surface. I guess if I had hit my head that hard on the street, I would have been killed. So I thought, well, I can lay here and let them count ten and get the $75,000 that was my guarantee, or I can get up and go for broke. One thing about it, my mind wasn't foggy, because I had done some tremendous training. I had walked something like nine or ten miles a day, and I had run at least that far each day. One time I went as much as sixteen miles, running and walking, just getting in shape, especially my legs, because it took me longer to get in condition at this stage of the game than when I was young. In those days I would usually get in shape in three weeks time, but this time it took me three months, but I did it well. I worked hard for that fight, unusually hard. I could have taken the easy way and been counted out. But then I thought about all the people I would be letting down—like my wife and children, my mother and auntie, other relatives and friends, my managers and trainers, myself, and the many fans I had. And the blacks who held their heads a little higher when I won. They had little enough to cheer about, and I would be taking that away from them. And then I thought about the racists who would be so happy and gloat and say how it was about time that black so-and-so got taken care of. So I decided to get up and go for broke and make a fight of it. The noise that Canadian crowd made was deafening. It sounded like the drone of a million bees in a small room. I had heard this once before—when I knocked Rocky Marciano down and almost won the heavyweight championship. Over the roar of the fans I could hear the referee, Jack Sharkey, shouting the count in my ear, his face so close that it looked grotesque, unreal. And I could hear my cornerman begging me to get up. I glanced from their anxious faces back to the impassive face of the referee, and I pushed myself to my feet. I got up full of insolence. I told myself I'd knock this guy out of the ring. Imagine him knocking me down, the champion of the world! Then, all of a sudden I was flat on my back again, and once again I looked up at the referee as he started counting. Then I thought: "This guy hits pretty hard. He hits funny with his little short right hook, and he bears watching. I better watch him very closely."

I had always known that I would come to the end of the road someday, because nobody lasts forever. But I always pictured myself going out the way a true champion

THE ARCHIE MOORE STORY

should—fighting, then carried out of the ring like a Viking warrior who had met his death in battle and is carried off the field on his shield. Well, it looked like I was going to be carried out all right, but what bothered me most was that I hadn't even landed a punch on Durelle. I didn't like to lose ever, you know, but if I had to, I wanted it to be like I had lost to Marciano, because that was a real fight, and when it was over, Rocky knew he had been in a battle, and the fans got their money's worth. So once again I staggered to my feet, and I came in with a left hook, and he split me with a right hand, and I went down again. My heels went up in the air, and I went loop-legged when I fell, and I thought: "Oh, my goodness, this guy *really can hit.*" And I began to pray softly to myself: "Oh, God, if I can just get to my corner, last this round and get to my corner. I don't mind losing this fight, but I got to hit this guy some punches. You know, I just can't lose this fight without at least hitting this guy once." It's funny the things you'll ask God to do for you under stress, when He's got His hands full with so many important things and you should really be asking what you can do to help Him. And then Auntie's poem went through my mind: "*When a task is once begun, never leave it until it's done; and if the labor is great or small, do it well or not at all.*" And I knew I had to get up. I knew that if I was going to teach this to youngsters and make it believable, I would have to believe in it myself— not just when things were going good, but also when things were tough. Whether I won or lost didn't matter anymore, but I had to get up and make a fight out of it. No fighter lasts forever, and here I was in my forties, so losing after all these years was excusable, but there was no excuse for a champion not putting up the best fight he possibly could.

So somehow I managed to get to my feet, and finally the bell rang, and I stumbled to my corner, and I passed right by my trainer. I didn't even see him, but he grabbed me and slapped my face real hard and gave me a whiff of spirits of ammonia, and he said, "Listen, stay away from this guy. This guy's dangerous. Do me this favor." I told him I could knock Durelle out, but he said, "Please do me this favor. We know you can knock him out, but it'll take a little bit longer. But *please* stay out of his way for a few rounds. Will you please do this? Box a little bit."

Jack Kearns, Dick Saddler and Barney Wright were in my corner. They looked me over and saw I didn't have any cuts, and then Kearns made me stand up. He said, "Look over there past Durelle's corner. Your wife and daughter are sitting over there and probably are worried sick about you. Wave at them to show you're okay." I couldn't see them, but I waved feebly, so Kearns said angrily, "Come on, wave like you're okay, not like you're dying. And give them a big smile." Well, he prodded me on until I was waving and smiling like everything was okay and I didn't have a care in the world.

What I didn't know was that Doc Kearns wanted me to stand up in my corner and wave and smile to take the wind out of Durelle's sails. It had nothing to do with my wife and daughter. And Doc told me later that when Durelle saw me standing and waving and smiling like an idiot, his jaw dropped about a foot, and he must have wondered what kind of guy he was fighting. Here he had knocked me down three times with his Sunday punches, and to all outward appearances it hadn't bothered me. That Kearns was a smart cookie, and he made sure that his fighter had everything going for him—even psychological warfare.

And I knew that he and Dick and Barney knew what

they were talking about, you know, so I took their advice and boxed for a few rounds and stayed out of trouble. Then, in the fifth round—because I had jarred him pretty good in the fourth round—I went in for the kill. But Durelle dropped me and knocked me loop-legged again. This time he hit me harder than in the first round, but by this time I was warmed up, you see, and I actually got up and outfought him the rest of that round, and that kind of took a little steam out of him.

In the sixth round I beat him again, and in the seventh I knocked him down. Then I began to see the fight change. After the seventh round I finally cut him to ribbons and beat him pretty good. In the tenth round I knocked him down again, and when the eleventh round opened I pounced out of my corner, swarmed all over him and knocked him out after forty-two seconds.

The Canadian crowd was somewhat subdued at this turnabout, seeing their hero lose, you know, and it took them a few seconds to get over their disbelief and shock, but to their credit, they applauded me for my comeback, and Durelle for his gameness and the great fight he had put up. They realized that they had seen a truly great fight between two worthy fighters—the kind of fight few fans get to see in their lifetime.

"That was a real hair-raiser," Lenny remarked. "By comparison, the Maxim fight must have been like a walk in the park."

"Well, Maxim was just defensive all the way, and he was just an unusually hard man to get to. Maxim's chief talent was defense. That's why he lacked color. But don't get me wrong. He was a very good fighter and hard to beat. He was a defensive fighter, and a good defensive fighter is the hardest in the world to beat. And I had my problems getting to him. As I mentioned before, I knocked him down only twice in three fights, although I did win all three. He was rugged, because I really hit him hard a lot of times."

"From what I've been able to dig up," Lenny said, "you've had 228 fights. Is that about right?"

"That's about right."

"You won 193 and drew in 8?"

"Yes."

"You won 140 by knockouts?"

"Right."

"That still stands as a world's record for knockouts, doesn't it?"

"Yes, I established the world's record when I knocked out Durelle, and that was my 127th knockout, which broke Young Stribling's record of 126, which had stood for thirty-three years. Since then I put thirteen more together on top of that to give it a little padding."

Fred Iverson, a good friend, had come in and sat down while I had been talking. "A little frosting on the cake," he said.

"Now," Lenny continued, "I also find that in 1962 you knocked out Alejandro Lavorante and Howard King, and you had a draw with Willie Pastrano."

I nodded.

"Prior to that, the last thing I have is that you were negotiating for a fight with Erich Schoeppner, the German champion, and if you won you were to get a fight with the winner of the Patterson-Johansson match. What happened there?"

"Well, I had been guaranteed $225,000 to fight Schoeppner, but during training I fell and sprained my wrist, so we asked for time for my wrist to heal, which would have been past the originally scheduled fight date. This gave them all the chance they needed to back down on the $225,000 guarantee."

"So you never fought Schoeppner?"

"No. My next fight was with Giulio Rinaldi in Italy, which I lost by a decision. Then the commissioner was on me for a title defense, so I signed for a rematch with Rinaldi in New York, in Madison Square Garden. That was my last title defense. It was in 1961. That was the time they said I couldn't make the weight, and that I was too old and too fat. Well, I took off twenty-eight pounds and made the weight, and I not only won the fight, but I proved that I could go fifteen rounds after I was way past forty. I went the full fifteen rounds and made him tired and exhausted at the end, and the only thing I got out of the fight was a blistered foot."

"I remember you had a heart problem that kept you out of the ring for a while. What was that all about?"

"This was in 1954," I replied. "I was weighing in to fight with a boy named Frankie Daniels, right here in San Diego, and the examining doctor refused to allow me to fight, saying I had a heart condition. So I went to a specialist and he told me that I did have some palpitation, or skipping of the heartbeat. He explained that in itself this was not dangerous, but that if it was not taken care of it could result in something serious. So I went to the hospital, rested and took medication, and eventually corrected this condition. Nine months later I went to Las Vegas and signed to fight Nino Valdes, the Cuban heavyweight, and I passed the test there. We went the full fifteen rounds, and I blacked Valdes' eyes and knocked him down and won the decision, so there was no more heart problem. Winning that fight put me right in line to fight Bobo

Olson, so I took off thirty-one pounds for Olson and knocked him out in the third round with a left uppercut. That was in June of 1955, and I weighed 186½."

"What did you think was your best fighting weight?"

"Probably my best fighting weight was about 185. I would feel comfortable, could move fast enough and could hit hard enough at that weight. Taking off a lot of weight always made me feel mean—mean at people I shouldn't have been mean with. I couldn't hardly stand anybody—not even my best friends—because I was just down to such an edge where I was uncomfortable to be around."

"Getting away from the fight game for a moment," Lenny said, "real far away, when did you first get the idea of ABC?"

"Well, ABC is an idea thirty-five years old, a boyhood dream now come true. We teach our boys to memorize the concept, and we teach the learner to teach as he learns."

"It's leadership by example," Mr. Iverson said.

"Really," I agreed. "Leadership by example. One man teaches twenty. Then that twenty teaches another twenty, and so on—and the thing mushrooms and grows. Of course, this is a starter. It's basic. Then I have to hand them to other people like yourself who can take them further.

"I have very strong feelings about the Any Boy Can program, because ABC is what the ghetto boy understands easily. ABC is what every boy should want to understand. Every person should want to be involved. Every person *is* involved in it whether he knows it or not. He should become actively involved in it. Am I right, Mr. Iverson?"

Mr. Iverson nodded agreement. "Our survival depends on the principles," he said.

"Right, right, right," I agreed, "because the beautiful principles of ABC are that every boy is involved in this thing, see? And it teaches the boy leadership potential— it seeks out the leadership potential in that boy. It surfaces the great potential that every youngster has in him. Unlimited, untold and unheard-of potential. I traveled to many school systems, and with the ABC procedure of getting these young people to respond, we surfaced a lot of great material in children. High school age, college age, with potential that has never really been surfaced. Many held back because they didn't know how to communicate with people. We teach them how to communicate with people."

"They are taught how to completely change their attitude toward life, toward school, toward their family," Mr. Iverson said. "I've read some beautiful letters from teachers noticing the difference in these ABC boys. It's a method of changing a negative attitude—negative because of the background, because of the conditions under which they live, the neglect and all—to a positive attitude."

EIGHT

•

I left town for several days on another good-will tour for the Boy Scouts and for the Any Boy Can organization, and when I returned I went to the ABC center, where a camera crew from the United States Information Agency was setting up to do a ten-day filming of ABC for overseas distribution. While waiting for them to set up, I got into the ring to spar a few rounds with Billy.

"A good fighter has to be a finisher," I told him. "When you've got a guy hurt you have to be able to go in and finish him off, because if you let him recover he might get you later on in the fight. Don't forget that when you're fighting the top fighters, they're in top condition, capable of a quick recovery if you let them, and after they've recovered it's a new fight and they could come back and take you out. The top fighters also know what to do when they're hurt. They will cover and clinch and back-pedal and get on their bicycle to stay out of the way until they recover. It's up to you to outsmart them no matter what they do. I'm going to pretend I'm a fighter who has just been hurt, and I want you to come after me. Okay, let's go!"

We assumed our fighting stances, and I danced back while Billy pursued. He trapped me in a corner, but just stood there looking at me, and I said, "Come on! Hit me! Hit me!"

Billy lashed out with a jab, but I quickly moved my head a few inches and the punch sailed harmlessly by. I took advantage of Billy's surprise by skipping by him and getting out of the corner. Billy turned to face me, but I said, "No, no, no! Much too slow. Not only were you wasting valuable time, but your defense was down. Even a man who was hurt can hit you when you turn like that." And I spent about fifteen minutes showing Billy, a fast learner, the proper way to pivot. We resumed the work-out and I danced and skipped from corner to corner, to the center of the ring and back to another corner with Billy always in relentless pursuit, coming closer and closer to landing a punch on me.

Finally I called time. "Good," I told Billy. "You were getting pretty close. A little more work and we'll have it. Remember—pursue, pursue, pursue. Don't let up on your man. If you want to be a champion, you've got to be a finisher. Like Jack Dempsey and Joe Louis."

We were standing in a corner of the ring and I was gently pressing Billy's stomach in while he took deep breaths. He was sweating and breathing much heavier than I, simply because I had made him do much more moving by proper maneuvering.

"You've really got to work that left jab," I said. "Then feint with your right and follow with a strong left hook to the body. A good, hard body shot will do more damage than one to the jaw. Try to hit your opponent high on the rib cage with a lot of zip. When you do, you will hamper his movements on whichever side you hit him, and then you can work on that side more freely. It has more effect than hitting a guy on the arm. Arms are a fighter's armor, so why waste punches on the armor? A hard punch to the stomach or upper part of the body has to hurt a fighter, no matter how well he has trained, because he can only develop a certain amount of toughness in those areas.

"A good jab is an absolute must if you want to be a good fighter. If you can't master a good jab, well, you might as well give it up. A good jab will keep your opponent off balance and enable you to maneuver. You can keep jabbing and pivoting on your left foot, making him take three steps to your one as he is forced to circle around you. And all this helps to wear a man down and frustrate him. I know it looks sensational to keep hitting a guy in the face, but believe me, it's body punching that wins fights. After your opponent has been softened up by stiff body punches, a shot to the jaw doesn't have to be nearly as hard to knock him out. Oh, it's true that some of the really hard hitters could take a guy out with one punch, but they're few and far between."

Suddenly I spotted Lenny at ringside and reached through the ropes to shake hands.

"He's looking real good," Lenny remarked.

"Yes," I agreed. "He has a lot to learn yet, but he's easy to teach. He picks things up in a hurry."

"What's going on?" Lenny asked, motioning toward the camera crew.

"They're making a documentary film about the Any Boy Can program for overseas distribution," I replied. "They're from the United States Information Agency."

"Great," he said. "The ABC is finally getting the recognition it deserves. When the U.S.I.A. takes an interest, you know you've arrived."

"Yes," I agreed. "It's very gratifying."

"How long will the filming take?"

"About ten days," I replied. "But don't worry, we'll still find some time to work on the book."

"Fine," Lenny said. "When can we get together?"

I thought for a moment, trying to remember my schedule, then I said, "Can you be at my house at six tonight? We can talk for a while, then if you want, you can go with me to a lecture I'm giving at a church in El Cajon."

"Real good," he agreed. "I'll see you at six."

Promptly at six that evening, Lenny showed up at my house, but I had arrived only a few minutes before and hadn't had a chance to eat my dinner. Lenny said he would make himself scarce until I had eaten, but I told him, "That's all right. Come on into the kitchen and we can talk while I eat."

So he accompanied me to the kitchen, where my wife, Joan, served me a plate of food.

"I'd like to hear a little more about some of your fights," Lenny began. "Particularly the fight with Rocky Marciano for the heavyweight championship."

Well, the Marciano fight was like a dream come true in that I had secured the match through a lot of letter-writing, convincing sportswriters that I deserved the match whether or not I was capable of winning it. A lot of supposedly knowledgeable people around had said that I wouldn't draw enough people to fill a telephone booth in a fight with Marciano. However, publicity opens many doors, proving the pen is mightier than the sword, so I hand-wrote about thirty-five letters a night for about two years until I finally got Marciano in a corner and people would ask him when he was going to fight me and he could no longer say, "I don't want to hurt that old man." I had built up such a backlog of impressive wins that he had either to fight me or face the embarrassment of refusal the rest of his fighting career.

Two of the most important people who helped open the door to this match were newspapermen. One was Dave Gregg out of Joplin, Missouri, a very fine writer and personal friend of mine; and the other was Dan Parker. Both have since passed away. Parker had always been a boxing stalwart who rode herd on the game, always fighting for fair play and honesty. The publicity brought response and the public began to write in. A public-opinion poll was conducted on whether I could beat Rocky Marciano. Only a few writers chose me to be the winner. One of these was Jack Murphy, the illustrious sports editor of the *San Diego Union*. And there was Dave Gregg and Bill Burns, about the only writers who saw me winning the fight.

So the fight was announced on television and radio and in the papers, and I began a publicity campaign of my own to stir up interest in the match. I promoted the Lucky Thompson dance band. Lucky was one of the all-time-great tenor-sax players. I bought a new Thunderbird and I took flying lessons from a fellow named George West in a Piper Cub. I was drawing eight hundred to nine hundred people a day to my training-camp workouts because of all this publicity I had been creating, so the sportswriters began to sit up and take notice and came to watch the workouts and write about me. One day a writer by the name of Gil Millstein decided he wanted to write a story on me—something with a different slant. So I took him up in a plane. I had a beautiful takeoff, but when I came in to land there was a stiff breeze that blew the plane sideways, so we had a rough landing and Gil said, "That was a nice landing. How long have you been flying?" I told him that it was my first flight, and the story he filed gave me more publicity. But Jim Norris ordered me not to fly any more, as there was already $700,000 in advance sales for the fight and he didn't want anything to happen to me.

The night of the fight, September 21, 1955, a hurricane came up from the Florida coast and was threatening to hit New York. However, it veered off and went to Cape Hatteras, but the fight was postponed until the next night. There were over 60,000 fans at the fight, including Humphrey Bogart and Burt Lancaster, who had come all the way from California to see me fight. And there was Lauren Bacall, General Douglas MacArthur, the Mayor of New York and many other notable people. Starting down the aisle, I was very confident, pleased that I was fighting for the heavyweight championship and that I had drawn such a big crowd; more than Marciano had drawn against Ezzard Charles or Jersey Joe Walcott by some 15,000. As I approached the ring, some fan said loudly, "Look at him. He looks like he's going to the electric chair." I felt like turning around and spitting in this guy's face for making a crack like that, because being afraid was the last thing in my mind. This was one fight that I had always wanted—a fight for the heavyweight championship of the world. I had worked hard to get this fight. I had wanted this fight very badly. Just as badly as I had wanted the Joey Maxim fight for the light-heavyweight championship, and here was this punk intimating that I was afraid.

We had argued with Marciano's managers about the amount of tape to be used to protect our fists. They only wanted to allow six feet of adhesive gauze instead of the usual ten feet, so we would be fighting with almost no protection on our hands, but I felt that if Marciano could stand it, so could I.

I entered the ring and sat in my corner, awaiting the introductions, and strangely enough the men in my corner seemed afraid, but I was excited and happy. This was a big night for me. I saw Marciano sitting in his corner across from me, and I saw his trainer reach down into the bucket and rub his hands inside the bucket, and I knew what was happening. He was taking Vaseline from the bucket and rubbing it on Marciano's neck and scalp and brows. This was so that blows would glance off, doing the least damage, and I pointed this out to my trainer and told him to go over and make them take the Vaseline off, but when he went over and complained to the referee, the referee ordered him to go back to my corner, so I said, "That's all right. I'll knock it off of him."

At the opening bell I came out of my corner to meet Marciano, and strangely enough he started backing away. This almost made me laugh, and I thought he must be afraid of me. I jabbed several times, but they went over Marciano's head, as he was boxing pretty low, so I thought I would change tactics and make him straighten up, because he was pretty hard to hit while in the crouch. So in the second round I feinted Marciano and took a half-step back, and as he followed me in with a short overhand right I took another short step backward so that he missed me by three inches and I came through with an uppercut that hit him right on the chin and he went down heavily on one knee and both elbows. The referee counted two over him and he got up and staggered to the ropes, placing both elbows over the ropes for support and glazedly staring out at the roaring fans, and the referee continued to count—which he was not supposed to do according to the rules then in effect. Once a fighter was back on his feet he was supposed to be on his own, and I felt that if I could have gotten him when he got up after the two count that I could have become the heavyweight champion. Rocky was a wide-open target at that point:

dazed, confused and with absolutely no defense—and no mobility. It would have been like hitting a punching bag.

My trainer was screaming, "Hit him! Hit him!" I moved in, but the referee stepped between us and grabbed Marciano's gloves, carefully and slowly wiping them off, and then he yanked Marciano to him, which may have helped snap him out of his fog. And all the while I was waiting impatiently to go in and finish Marciano off. But it was too late, for Marciano, being the great fighter that he was, had by now recovered enough from his dazed condition. He threw a wild right that caught me in the back of the neck. Then I began to fight his fight, because I became stupid with anger and tried to get rid of him. I abandoned my fight plan completely. In the third round I threw caution to the winds, because Marciano was really throwing leather. The fight was full of action. It was one of my best fights, but eventually Marciano got to me, knocking me out in the ninth round.

I don't think that there is a fighter, past, present or future, who could slug it out with Marciano and come out on top. Rocky did say that I was one of the toughest men he had ever fought, and that the punch I landed on his jaw was one of the hardest he had ever received. He said that he felt it for years afterward—every time he would think of our fight. That was Marciano's last fight. He retired soon after that, and I was greatly saddened when he was killed in an airplane crash. Rocky was a truly great champion, a gentleman, a good friend and a fine human being—a real credit to the boxing game and to the world, and we will all miss him. My championship fight with him is a bout I will always cherish. It was a game effort and a great fight, but I could not close my books in this manner, so I continued fighting, and as my record shows, I did very well even though I was regarded as an "old man,"

which I was as far as boxing is concerned, winning the
Boxer of the Year award when I was in my forties.

I finished my dinner and repeated my invitation for
Lenny to accompany me to the lecture, to which he readily agreed. I hurriedly dressed, wearing a pair of white
dress ABC coveralls with the ABC emblem over one
pocket and my name over the other. We then went to the
ABC center, where we picked up Director Lake and several of the ABC boys and then proceeded in three cars to
the church in El Cajon.

NINE

•

On our arrival we were warmly welcomed by church officials and conducted to a classroom jammed with adults and children. In a few minutes the camera crew from the U.S.I.A. arrived, and for a little while there was considerable confusion while they set up their cameras, lights and audio equipment. When everything was ready, an official of the church made the introduction and I stepped to the front of the classroom to the accompaniment of gratifying applause. I introduced the U.S.I.A. crew and Director Lake and Lenny. Then I said, "I am on the road most of the time for the Boy Scouts of America trying to develop a program that is mighty important to young people. We feel that in order for a youngster to cope with what is happening today, he must be made to feel important—for eventually we will depend on these youngsters. We teach them in the home, in church and in school, and all these are important in a child's life. In my travels throughout the country, I have found out how to get into the inner minds of young people. I have been touring the country from Maine to New Mexico, from Florida to California, and all stops in between—Kalamazoo, Grand Rapids and all of these places—and this makes me feel good, because I feel that I am helping people. I would like to involve some young people in this room in some things that will test their alertness." I then proceeded to select children of various ages from the audience and asked them to come on the stage. Finally they were all grouped in front of me.

"We will first start off with a typical ABC procedure to test the reflexes of these bright young people," I said.

Suddenly the smile was gone from my face and replaced by a stern look as I changed from Archie Moore the lecturer to Archie Moore the instructor. "Now," I told the children on the stage. "I want you to listen to me. Listen to me and *hear* me. All of you. Because you are involved in this program. In a group like this there is always a leader. Whoever he is, it doesn't matter to me. I don't care. All right. You are to go to the corner of the room, and when I clap my hands I want the tallest member of your group to stand here in front of me. Then the next tallest must line up next to him and so on down the line until you are all out here on the stage lined up with your feet wide apart to resemble an A and your hands at your sides. Understood?"

The children nodded agreement and went to the designated corner.

I turned to the audience. "Everyone in this room—*everyone* in this room has a part in this. The part that you will play is the judge, and I'll soon tell you your function." Then I turned to the children huddled in the corner and clapped my hands. "Go!" I commanded. "Come on, move out. Let's go!"

The children filed out quickly and lined up by size, but their alignment was a bit ragged.

"Come on," I urged. "Straighten it up. Make the line straight."

Suddenly the stern look left my face and was replaced with a broad smile. "Good," I approved. "This only took about fifteen seconds. And remember, this is the first time I have ever met these young people in my life. I think they did very well. Give them a round of applause, will you?"

The audience complied, and when the applause died down, I said, "Now, feeling that I know these young people are interested in what we have to say, we'll go on. Let me see if I can trap these young people into spelling the wrong way. I am going to give them easy, basic words to relax them, and all of you people in the audience, as I mentioned before, are the judges. Now, I don't want you to laugh at them and embarrass them. We don't want any of these young people to be embarrassed. All I want you to do when they miss is say, 'Sorry about that.' Let's hear you say it."

"Sorry about that," the audience chorused.

"Good," I said. Then I turned to the children lined up on the stage. "Any of you want to sit down?"

"No," came the unanimous response.

"Of course not. Because nobody wants to hear the audience say what?"

"Sorry about that!" the children replied.

I went down the line, giving the children words to spell, and a few of them missed and sat down.

"Now," I went on. "We're going to talk about an animal. And this animal is fierce. He's a terrible animal at times, and this animal is a lion." Turning to one of the children, I said, "Spell 'lion'."

The child complied, and I went down the line naming different animals for the children to spell, always giving the more difficult words to the older children and the easier words to the younger ones, and when the children did well, I frequently turned to the audience and asked for a round of applause for them.

"All right," I said after several rounds of spelling, "we're going to imagine we're very hungry, and we're going to name different fruits, and if anybody repeats a fruit previously mentioned, he is out of the game. Understood?"

The children then went down the line, calling out the names of different fruits. At first it was easy, but it became increasingly difficult to avoid repetition as the game went on, and several more of the children were eliminated.

"Now," I said, "we ate our dessert first, and this is all right, because we were hungry, but we're still hungry, and we walk and we walk and we walk until finally we get to a restaurant, and they have many kinds of food there. I want you to tell me what you would order, but you can't order something that anybody else has ordered or you're out."

And again they went down the line, and eventually more children were eliminated.

It was interesting to see how this game changed the shy, timid ones into confident, assured children in a matter of moments. When I would come to a boy who nervously mumbled his answer while staring at the floor, I would say, "Come on! Speak up! Look at the audience!" My voice would be stern, and when the boy obeyed he would be rewarded by a big smile and a pat on the head.

I turned to the audience. "These children have been up here quite a while," I said. "And it is very important that people be able to appear before the public and speak, and this is one of the objectives of games like this. Another objective is to activate their brains, to teach them to think. For all these young people have the ability—but it must be brought to the surface—by games, which is something all children understand; and by competition, because everybody likes to win. And later in life, when their minds have learned to think, and when they have built up their confidence, it will be easier for them to achieve whatever goal they desire.

"Now," I went on, "we have three winners. Three who survived the various tests we put them through." And with a wave of my hand I indicated the three children still standing on the stage. "There is a great thrill and much satisfaction in being a winner, whether it's in a little contest like this or something much greater, and this satisfaction and thrill is a thing that motivates people to do great things. So these little games are just a beginning, but we have to begin somewhere. The competition is good. Winning is great.

"All of life is a competition, so what better time is there to teach this than in childhood. And what better time is there to teach them how to get the most out of their brilliant little minds? And what better time is there to get the feeling of satisfaction there is in winning? To develop the winning habit."

Turning to the three remaining children, I said, "I want you to give me your names—loud and clean and clear."

The first girl gave her name.

"And how old are you?"

"Thirteen," she replied, loud and clear. Her tone and posture was that of an assured, confident young lady, a striking contrast to the frightened, shy, timid girl who had come to the stage just a short time before.

"Thirteen," I said. "Very good. And what do you want to be in life?"

"I want to be a music teacher."

"Music teacher? This is beautiful. Now, do you mind singing me a song?"

She didn't hesitate. She sang and received generous applause for her efforts.

I then turned to the next in line, and the boy gave his name and his age, eleven.

"And what do you want to be in life?" I asked,

"A doctor."

"Very good. I'm going to ask you to sing a song. I know you can do it. Any song you want to sing, but make it loud and clean and clear."

Again the psychology worked and the boy sang his song loud and clear and was rewarded by applause from the audience. Then I turned to the third child and asked her her name, and when she replied, I said, "What a beautiful name. And what a beautiful child. What do you want to be when you grow up?"

"A missionary."

"A missionary? Very fabulous work, and much needed. You have passed all the tests so far and are one of our three remaining contestants, and I want you to sing a song for us."

The girl sang, then she received a round of applause and a rewarding smile from me.

I turned to the audience. "I'd like to say, ladies and gentlemen, mothers and fathers, brothers and sisters—it wasn't that I expected any startling singing up here. I just wanted to show you that all children have the courage. All they need is a little help to bring it out—to encourage it. I guarantee you it would be difficult to ask somebody to come out of the audience and sing for us, but these children have learned to conquer a thing we call fear through the games we played.

"Now, as I place my hand over each of these three young people, you will applaud for the one you thought best. I am not the judge. You are the judges, and you will judge fair and square."

The applause for all three was enthusiastic and evenly distributed. After several tries there was still no apparent difference in the amount of applause, so I decided to call it a three-way tie. I took their names and promised to send each of them a gift. Then the children took their seats.

"Now, remember," I said, "these are children from your own community. And these are great young people. We have some young people in our community that we think are pretty great too. We're from the inner city, the so-called ghetto, and, of course, the ghetto is only a state of mind, because there are some great young people in the inner city—great young people. All they need is training and they can do anything anybody else can do.

"I have some young people we call the ABC—Any Boy Can. When I found these young people, a lot of them were sniveling, half-cowards—not being cowards themselves, but forced to be by circumstances. Who knows? Maybe somebody in this room has felt the toe of somebody else's boot, or a strap on his back. I'm not a stranger to this myself, but I rose above it in spite of everything, and I'm trying to keep my young people from being the recipients of this type of treatment. I'm teaching them moral, spiritual and physical self-defense values so that they can walk like other men and be proud. Instructor Lake saw the youngsters work one day and he told me that he would very much like to learn this. He was an all-star basketball player, and one day he told me that if he'd had this kind of instruction when he was young there was no telling what he might have been." Then I said, "I would like to have Student Randall bring the ABC boys up in front. He will be their leader."

The ABC boys filed up on the stage and quickly lined up.

Student Randall said, "Good evening, students."

"Good evening, Instructor Randall," the students replied.

"Say good evening to the audience."

"Good evening, audience."

"We will now salute the flag. Atten*shun!*"

With military precision their feet came together, their right hands were placed over their hearts and as one man they gave the Pledge of Allegiance with emphasis and feeling. Then they demonstrated the ABC concept and were warmly applauded by the deeply impressed audience. I congratulated them on a job well done and asked them to take their seats.

"Training these young people was not easy," I said. "But it was a lot of fun because it was a challenge every day. And with Instructor Lake coming in and taking over, this was great, as he has a lot more to offer in a different way. I can only offer a foundation on which to build. If we can make all our young people feel important and unafraid, they can go into any areas they like. They can get an education and take advantage of opportunity. There are a lot of children who fail because they don't have the courage of their convictions. We try to give them that courage because we know that Any Boy Can— that means girls too. You've got to push them a little bit. There is so much potential in young people that even their parents don't know about. Sometimes a child doesn't communicate with his parents. They would rather communicate with somebody across town. They would rather communicate with a dear friend.

"If we could communicate together we could break up all this race disorder and disunity. We could have a very fine society, because as far as I'm concerned, there are elements that make up so-called races of people. I'd rather call them nations of people. There are only five faces on this earth. Five faces, which are represented by five fingers." I held up my right hand and pointed at each finger with my left forefinger. "Five faces," I repeated. "Black, white, red, yellow, brown. There are no more. *These are the five faces of man.* And each of these faces must be in harmony with the others. Like notes of the musical scale—and anybody who has ever studied music knows—the lines spell E-G-B-D-F, and we learn this by the phrase 'Every Good Boy Does Fine.' And this is true. Every good boy does fine. Black, white, red, yellow, brown. But like music, they must be in harmony. One note by itself is just a tinkle, but a chord has harmony.

"Let's go a step further. When we are taught music we are taught to remember the spaces between the lines of a musical score by the simple word "face"—FACE. So from this the meaning is clear. There are but five faces of man, and they must live together in harmony. Each face by itself is worth only 20 percent, so it takes all five faces to work together to get power. But, of course, the real power comes from God above. We know this. We know where the power comes from. We get our spiritual power and motivation from up above.

"I wrote an article several months ago and said that the devil is at work. And he *is* at work. The devil can be many faces of people. He can have five faces. He could be black, white, red, yellow or brown. The devil could be you. If any man feels that he is better than another man because he is a different color, he is a racist. There are black racists and there are white racists, so let us all work

together and make America a strong place, a place where
we can live together in brotherhood. This is what I'm
talking about. I feel that many people have died—too
many people have died—trying to prove that they are
better than others. Let's get together and work in harmony. We can make America a strong place, a place in
which all of us could be proud to live happily together.
And in closing I would like to say that it has been enjoyable to watch these young faces, to have these young people involve themselves in the ABC program and to have
the ABC boys here to meet you. We must help these
young people to help themselves. We thank you very
much."

Every day ABC is becoming better-known both here
and abroad. I have appeared before thousands and before
mere handfuls. But I keep punching away, just as I did in
the ring—because that's what it takes to be a winner.

In February of 1968 the ABC received the Freedom
Foundation's patriotism award, a special citation for
"Providing a challenge for youth to become contributing
members of their communities and upholding the ideals
and ideas that were present at the founding of our great
nation."

The Freedom Foundation grants awards for "outstanding achievement in bringing about a better understanding
of the American way of life."

TEN

•

In ABC, one of the ways we reward the boys when they do good work is by taking them on what we call a "function." These functions are trips, sometimes far and sometimes near, but no matter the distance, the boys love them. It takes them away from the depressing ghetto environment they live in, even if only for a short while, and shows them that there is a different kind of life they can lead if they are willing to work for it.

One such function was arranged and paid for by Fred Iverson, a good friend of the ABC. This trip was to the Pala Indian reservation, and it was both a heartwarming and heartbreaking experience. Heartwarming because of the obvious happiness it brought to the boys, and heartbreaking to see a close-up of how little they had. It's like reading about hundreds of people being killed in an earthquake in a far-off land. It's not nearly as much of a shock as personally witnessing one person killed before your eyes.

As many times as I have been in close-up situations with these boys, I can never help feeling bad about their problems. These are ghetto children, many of them from fatherless homes and all of them in the very low-income group. In the close proximity of the bus ride to Pala, they talked to each other, revealing their secret dreams and wishes. Many of their desires were just for the simple things, things that children from families in better financial circumstances take for granted—like a few pennies in their pocket to be able to buy an ice-cream cone, a candy bar or a bag of potato chips. Some of their desires were much greater—like wishing they had a father, or dreaming of a college education, or becoming a great athlete, or becoming rich so that they could help their families. In short, to achieve importance and stature.

We were to leave at three-thirty in the afternoon, and the bus was outside the ABC center. Director Lake called all the boys together inside the center for a final word. "All right fellows," he said. "I want you to pay attention to what I am going to say. Any of you do anything out of line up there, I'm going to warn you once, and just once. The next time you get out of line I'm going to put you in the bus, and that's where you'll stay until we get back here. Understood?"

"Yes, sir!" they chorused.

"Okay, into the bus!"

The boys filed into the bus in an orderly fashion and we were on our way. It was a heavily overcast afternoon and shortly after we started it began to drizzle, but the weather failed to dampen their joy and enthusiasm. They soon began singing, and their singing had a beautiful, haunting Negro-spiritual quality with the underlying sadness of an oppressed people. Soon one of the older boys took over and divided the singers into three groups—the front, middle and rear of the bus. He then announced that the three groups would have a contest, with Director Lake to be the judge. At the finish of each contest, Lake would announce the winner. Here was a good example of how the ABC training was paying off. Lake's word was law; nobody disputed his decision, but instead all applauded the winners and just tried harder to win on the next round.

It was still drizzling lightly when we arrived at the Pala Indian reservation, and we were welcomed by the Pala Indians and a Boy Scout group from the area. A reporter and photographer from the *San Diego Union* were also there. The reservation grounds were both immaculate and picturesque. The historical buildings were well-kept —some being the original ones, while others had been restored. There was an outdoor shrine, a large aviary, an inside chapel and a museum, and of particular interest was the graveyard with the strange epitaphs on markers and tombstones dating back to the early nineteenth century.

The Pala Indians were very friendly and pleasant, although many of our ABC boys were taken aback by the fact that instead of wearing Indian garb such as feathered headdresses, moccasins and buckskin, they were dressed just like we were. I busied myself outside, frying chicken on a grill that had been placed on top of a steel drum within which a log fire roared. When I finished, the boys helped me take the chicken to the assembly room, where the Indian women had been dishing up their own fried chicken, Indian bread, potato salad, beans, coffee and dessert. Finally, when everybody had eaten and the room was cleaned up, the ABC boys conducted their concept under the leadership of Director Lake. When they finished, I was introduced and addressed the gathering.

"I thought," I began, "when I was young that I would like to do something to help my brothers, my neighbors. Who are my neighbors? Every man is my neighbor. We are all responsible for one another. So I developed and taught a program that I felt would benefit young people. A program that would give the youngsters a chance to think for themselves and identify with something." I indicated the ABC boys lined up on the stage, then said, "These young men possess something you can't see outwardly, but it's inside of them. It's a great heart—a courageous heart and a competitive spirit. We teach these young men the right way to go in life. Instructor Lake has done a wonderful job with these young men. I have been working for the Boy Scouts for nearly a year now, and I have never lost my love for ABC, because I know that ABC will develop boys, and I'm going to help develop them, but I need help. Men like Instructor Lake.

"ABC is a starter, and this is what we want—to start our young people off with their best foot forward. And once we get a boy started with his best foot forward, it is easy to communicate with him and guide him in the right path, and I venture to say that since I've been here with these young men they have gotten into very little trouble. Of course, boys will get into little scrapes, but by and large they have done wonderfully well. I think that Boy Scouting is a wonderful thing, and I hope that eventually we will merge.

"Our boys can really defend themselves from a physical standpoint. They can also defend themselves from a mental standpoint and a moral standpoint. Because we teach them this. And we motivate them. If they get good grades in school and behave themselves, we reward them with functions such as this. We take them many places. I have had boys with me to Washington, D.C., Las Vegas, Seattle, San Francisco, Disneyland and many other places.

"We try to change the attitudes of young people from negative to positive. We want them to think, to dream, to want to be somebody. And a lot of them will achieve their goals. One of them may be a mayor. Who can tell? I hope one of them becomes President of the United States. They may not make that, but I'll guarantee you that most of them will stay out of jail, and this is the main thing. We want them to stay out of jail. We want them to do the right thing, and we would like very much to invite all of our little mission friends to join ABC, Boy Scouting, YMCA or Boys' Club of America. We would like them to join any club they would like to join. We would like them to make their own choice. Let them think for themselves. All of you young adults should work with these boys and help them, because they need help to bring their latent abilities to the surface.

"We've had a fine time here and I hope you'll invite us back, and I hope that you will come to San Diego and visit us."

Functions such as the one to the Pala Indian reservation really serve two purposes. Not only are they rewards for the boys, but they give us a chance to showcase the ABC and thus get others interested in the program. Of course, these trips are expensive and would not be possible if it were not for our many, many friends—far too numerous to mention—who donate their time, services and money. I would like to tell you about the Moceri family, however, as their story is one that I feel could only happen in America. At the age of eight years, Sam Moceri was selling supplies to ships in Italy, where he was born. He also bought and sold fish, until at the age of fourteen he had earned enough to pay his passage to America. His father had come to the United States in 1890, and when Sam Moceri arrived, his father gave him $100 with the warning that he was now on his own.

Sam began peddling vegetables in Detroit, Michigan, but was not doing too well. Then one day he discovered a better way to make money. He had been peddling all

morning and had sold only one bunch of bananas. He
stopped at a grocery store to buy a loaf of bread and at
the same time sold two bunches of bananas to the store.
Thus began his prosperous career as a produce whole-
saler. Eventually, he decided to sell out and go to the
West Coast. On the West Coast he ventured into the
soda-water business, the cannery business, opened a bar
and a liquor store—and eventually went broke. He had to
start all over again, so he decided to go back to the business he knew best—the produce business, this time in
San Diego, where he prospered once more and was
joined in the business by his brother Nick and his sons,
Sal and Dominic. The Moceris have been good friends of
the ABC and poverty-stricken people in the San Diego
area. Many times they have given me cases of fruits and
vegetables, which I distribute to needy families.

And there is Fred Iverson, a retired business execu-
tive who is always around to help ABC when we need
him.

And Gerald Awes, Chairman of the Board of Lucky
Stores, who, convinced that Any Boy Can was reaching
youngsters who were not being served by other youth organizations, made personal contributions and also convinced Lucky Stores to support us ever since we started
in San Diego. And all this went unpublicized, as Mr.
Awes did not want anyone to feel that these contributions were commercially oriented and feels that the success of ABC should come from strong local support.

And there are a great many other people and organizations who have given us this kind of positive help. Knowing people like this makes it all worthwhile for me. Spade
Cooley, for instance. Many of you probably remember
Spade as "The King of Western Swing." He was a violin-

ist and set a new style with his band by combining western and popular swing music and for seven years appeared seven nights a week on a Los Angeles radio
station. In 1947 he became a star of television, appearing
on KTLA's "Spade Cooley" show, a program that was
rated No. 1 in Los Angeles for four years and won numerous awards. Then, at the height of his career, Spade was
sent to prison. He developed heart disease and was sent
to Vacaville, where I met him on a visit. We struck up an
immediate friendship, and I found him to be humble and
understanding, a kind man, and I asked him to help me
with a song I was writing. He readily agreed, and with
the help of Glenn Sherley, we wrote a song titled "It's
Time To Live," and it goes like this:

> Well, it's time to live before it's time to die;
> time to smile before it's time to cry; but it's
> those people who just won't try that keeps on
> a-bothering me. Well, things look bad, but they
> gotta get better; if we have enough faith and all
> pull together; there ain't enough love in this
> world for each other, and that's what's a-
> bothering me. Take a lot of love, mix it with the
> sunshine, have a big smile and it'll work a won-
> der sometime. Keep your very best foot forward
> all the time; set your goal and you're sure to
> climb. Yes, it's time to live before it's time to
> die; time to smile before it's time to cry; but it's
> those people who just won't try that keeps on
> a-bothering me. Everyone of us has got to do
> our part—give of yourself and let it come from
> the heart, but it's those people who just won't
> start that keeps on a-bothering me.

Those lyrics carry a beautiful message. Shortly after we

finished that song, Spade received his parole, and the Alameda County Sheriff's Department asked Spade if he would perform for them at a benefit for widows and orphans in Oakland, California, on November 19, 1969. Spade agreed, and little did he realize what a fateful day that would turn out to be. He was nervous about how people would accept him, and he wrote telling me of these anxieties and asked if I would go with him, as he would then feel better and more at ease, so I went to Oakland. His son Donnie and his daughter Melody also went to Oakland, and I don't know of anything that could have made Spade happier.

During rehearsal, all the other performers and stagehands stopped to listen to Spade play his violin. He played with great beauty and feeling that came from his heart, and everybody applauded. Still, Spade was nervous about how the public would accept him, so I said, "Spade, these people aren't coming here to hear you confess about something you did years ago. You served your time for that. Nobody's even going to mention it."

So Spade was reassured, and after Chill Wills introduced him he summoned up his courage and said to the audience, "Ladies and gentlemen, I've come here because I want to make a comeback, and I want to assure you I can, and I want to dedicate my first number to a man who helped me when I needed it—Cowboy Bob Wills of the Texas Playboys." And then Spade played "San Antonio Rose," and he put everything he had into it. He played so fantastically that everybody in the audience—and the other performers and the stagehands—all stood up and cheered. Spade was so overwhelmed that his hand went to his eyes to brush away a tear. And it's a good thing the applause lasted for as long as it did, because it gave him a chance to compose himself.

He thanked the audience when they finally sat down, then he said he would like to sing the song written by him and Glenn Sherley and me, and he asked me to come out and sing it with him, and we sang "It's Time To Live," and again the audience went wild.

Spade finished his performance with two more numbers. Believe me, the adrenaline was really flowing and he was one happy guy. All in one day, his children and the public had accepted him again, and their enthusiasm was beyond his wildest dreams. When he was through, he said he was going out to get a breath of fresh air. I was backstage signing autographs when suddenly somebody ran up to me and screamed that Spade was out in the hall and that he was dying. I rushed back to the hall, but found that somebody had dragged Spade into a room and that everybody was standing around him, holding his hands and crying. His face was pale and his lips blue, and he looked like he was dead, but I ordered everybody to stand back and straddled him and gave him artificial respiration like I had learned from the Boy Scouts. Then he began to breathe, and pretty soon his breathing became regular and he opened his eyes, but I knew they weren't seeing, as they had that dead, fishy stare. When his eyes closed I gave him a heart massage. His eyes opened again, and this time he looked at me and gave me a half-smile in recognition. Just then somebody came in with an oxygen inhalator, but in the excitement they put it on sideways and his breathing was impaired. He passed out again, so I gave him another heart massage. He opened his eyes once more and again gave me that half-smile of recognition. Then an ambulance from the hospital came and they took him away. I called the hospital a little later, but they told me he was dead on arrival.

Here is a man who went out with a standing ovation

after a splendid performance in his chosen field after being reconciled with his son and daughter. He died in peace and harmony, and this is beautiful.

Many times people tell me I'm out of my mind to work as hard as I do when I could make a fortune by taking advantage of the name I have built up by going into something lucrative—like movies, television, boxing or business—and work about half as hard as I do now. Granted I could have made a lot of money, and with much less work, but believe this: The beautiful experiences I've had, and the beautiful people I've met, are worth all the money there is.

I want to give you just one more example of what I mean, then you can judge for yourself whether my choice was right.

Late in 1968 I made an appearance at Los Amigos High School in Santa Ana. Los Amigos is a beautiful new school, built with state aid, and is a brand-new concept in schools. None of the classrooms have doors, and the rooms and corridors are carpeted so that the sound of people walking around does not disturb the class. If a student has any free time, he can drop in on any class he wishes and there is no disturbance, as there are no doors to open and close; and another advantage is that the students don't feel cooped up, which several teachers told me makes for happier and more attentive students. Being a low-budget school, every detail was well-planned to make the best use of the available funds and space. The gymnasium—which also doubles as an assembly room—has bleachers that fold against the wall, and the lunchroom can readily be converted into a small auditorium. The students are from the lower-third income group, and integrated. During my appearance there in 1968 I conducted one of my "thinking game" contests and the win-

ner was a blind white girl, Stephanie Miller, a courageous
girl with both outer and inner beauty. But let me quote
from a couple of letters I received after that appearance.

One reads:

> It was a privilege to be in attendance at Los
> Amigos High School when you presented your
> ABC program. You were truly outstanding. I
> was so impressed with your personal touch with
> kids that I can't compliment you highly enough.
> The finale was one of the most inspirational
> events of my life. I sat and cried as you so
> gently, sincerely and warmly talked with the
> blind girl and got her to sing. That truly was
> magnificent, and you were so perceptive to the
> entire meeting and situation.
>
> Archie, keep up the good work, because your
> potential is unlimited. Los Amigos students, as
> well as all the adults in the audience, are better
> people because of your giving of yourself last
> Friday.

And another:

> As for the student assembly, I cannot find the
> words that adequately express my appreciation
> for the superb program you put on. In my
> twenty-one years in this school district, I have
> never witnessed a more genuine expression of
> affection between students and artist, or a more
> effective lesson in the art of developing charac-
> ter in young people. The youngsters and Los
> Amigos, especially Stephanie Miller, will re-
> member that assembly for years to come, as I
> certainly shall.

Early in 1970 I again found myself in Santa Ana, so I asked Ken Hickenbottom, a Boy Scout official, if he could arrange for me to go back to Los Amigos and talk to my friends. This was at 11:30 A.M. A few minutes later, Ken told me that an assembly was all set for twelve-fifteen. The kids gave me a standing ovation when I was introduced. Believe me, there is no thrill to match this kind of acceptance.

After a short talk I asked for volunteers to compete in my "thinking game" contest. Before long I had about thirty contestants of different races, and I was happy to see that my little friend Stephanie Miller, now prettier than ever, had volunteered to take part. The contestants were reduced to just four and were asked to sing. When they finished, the winner was chosen by the applause of the students, and this time it was a little black girl—and mind you, she was chosen by a predominantly white group of students. Stephanie, who had been eliminated earlier, was the first to come out and congratulate the winner. Then she turned to the audience and asked them for more applause for the new champion. She was on my right and the black girl on my left, and I grasped their hands. There we stood, a black man, a black girl and a white girl, and I said to the students, "This is beautiful. I'm tremendously proud of each and every one of you. You were absolutely colorblind in your choice of a winner, and that's as it should be. Now," I continued, "I'm going to give you something. Something that will help you the rest of your lives." I gave them Auntie's little poem:

When a task is once begun, never leave it until it's done. If the labor is great or small, do it well or not at all.

The assembly then disbanded and a group of youngsters surrounded me—some wanting autographs, some wanting answers and some wanting me to repeat Auntie's poem so they could write it down. So many of them asked about the poem that it proved to me that young people today are desperately searching for something worthwhile to latch on to, and it's up to us adults to fulfill this need. The questions these kids asked were not frivolous ones. Of course, there are always some who want to know about my boxing career, but by and large the questions were profound and showed an interest in and knowledge of what's happening in the world. After visiting with these kids and many others like them, I'm not worried about America's future, especially if we adults do our part to help guide them along the right path.

As I was signing autographs and answering questions, Stephanie appeared in front of me. She grasped my hand in hers, her unseeing eyes moist and her beautiful voice husky with emotion as she said, "God bless you, Archie Moore."

I felt a little lump in my throat and a chill race down my spine, but I swallowed the lump and managed to say, "Thank you, Stephanie. And may God bless you."

I don't know of any other kind of work that would give me the satisfaction of changing youngsters from juvenile delinquents to good, solid citizens. And I don't know of any other kind of work I could do where a wonderful girl like Stephanie Miller would walk up to me and say, "God bless you, Archie Moore."

ELEVEN

●

There has always been a bit of controversy about my age. My mother says I was born on December 16, 1913, but I say I was born on December 13, 1916. Maybe I was three years old when I was born, and if that's so, then I should know.

I was born in Benoit, Mississippi, the son of Mr. and Mrs. Thomas Wright. My mother, Lorena, was only seventeen years old when I was born, and she had previously given birth, at the age of fifteen, to a daughter, Rachel. The responsibilities proved to be too great for my parents, who were just barely out of their own childhood, and they separated when I was eighteen months old.

My uncle and aunt, Mr. and Mrs. Cleveland Moore, then took on the responsibility of raising me and my sister, you see, and my name was changed from Archie Lee Wright to Archie Lee Moore to avoid any problems in the years to come. I never held it against my mother for turning Rachel and me over to our aunt and uncle to be raised. She just did what she had to, you understand. This thing of teen-agers getting married seldom works, because young love, while it is beautiful, you know, it just isn't enough in most cases to make a lasting marriage, as marriage is a serious business, and so many times love flies out the door when the bills start flying in and there isn't any money to pay them. Survival is tough, and I feel that a man should be reasonably secure before taking on the added responsibility of a wife and children. Oh, I know that teenage marriage has worked for some, and there isn't anything quite as beautiful as young love and romance—it's groovy, as the youngsters say—but it's hazardous. I know it didn't work for me, so you see, I can readily understand the predicament my mother found herself in.

Uncle Cleveland and Aunt Willie Pearl Moore lived in St. Louis, where they had migrated for economic reasons, and it was in St. Louis that I spent my childhood. As I grew up I came to idolize my uncle and wanted to be like him. Uncle Cleveland was a husky, hardworking man who worked steadily as a laborer six days a week, never complaining, and spent Saturday nights playing cards and having a drink or two with the boys. He relaxed on Sunday and went back to work again on Monday to earn a living for his family. We lived well due to his industrious work habits.

Uncle Cleveland was an extremely well-developed man. He had broad, heavily muscled shoulders, a huge, deep chest and tremendous arms and legs. I remember how I used to love to watch his muscles ripple as he washed up before dinner. Those rippling muscles would fascinate and almost hypnotize me. I wanted muscles just like his. I wanted to be as strong as my uncle. I worked hard to develop my body, chinning myself, walking on my hands and doing push-ups, and the strength I built up played a big part in my success as a boxer. I think my uncle was just the finest man I have ever known.

I adore my auntie, a beautiful woman, a religious woman with high moral principles, a wise woman who

worked hard at teaching me right from wrong. Although
she never had children of her own, she was a great
mother in every sense. She gave us love and affection and
taught us all the things a good mother should teach her
children, so between my uncle and my aunt I was in-
fluenced greatly spiritually, physically, mentally and mor-
ally. They were a great inspiration to me.

My sister and I spent our summer vacations with our
grandparents in Mississippi, where we had cousins of our
own age to play with, and we really enjoyed these vacations. The house we lived in was old, you know, but my
grandfather was a farmer who owned his own land, and
there was always plenty of good food on the table. We
enjoyed such delights as chicken, pork, corn, cantaloupe,
fresh butter and watermelon that had been cooled in the
well, and we enjoyed the other pleasures of country life—
swimming and wading in the creek and hiking through
the pleasant countryside.

Until I was eight years old, I was not aware of the inequities and prejudices against black people, but this was
quite vividly brought to my attention in an incident that I
have not forgotten to this day. It was a sunny, clear and
pleasantly warm summer morning, and I was riding bare-
back on an old horse that belonged to my grandfather,
clutching desperately to the horse's mane while my sister
and cousin led the plodding horse down the dusty country road. The fields were green, the trees were in full
bloom, as were the wild flowers that abounded, and the
vast spaces without a sign of human habitation gave me a
feeling of freedom that I did not enjoy in crowded St.
Louis. The sweet scent of the flowers and greenery were
heady and this city boy was transformed into a knight
wearing shining armor—a knight whom King Arthur had
ordered to slay the dragon and rescue the damsel in dis-

tress. In my gauntleted right hand I held my long lance,
and at my left side was my gleaming sword, and I sat
straight and tall in the saddle, the purple plume in my
helmet waving gently. My horse was not a plodding old
gray horse, you understand, head lowered and jerking
with each step—he was a shining black horse in elegant
trappings, and his head was proudly held high as he
pranced along the road.

My beautiful reverie was suddenly shattered as a white
boy leaped from behind a bush and with a switch made
from a tree branch lashed at the old horse's rump. The
horse, startled, reared up and I was thrown to the ground.
My reflexes were good even then, you see, and I quickly
rolled out of the way of the flailing hoofs, jumped to my
feet, grasped the white boy and shook him roughly. I was
infuriated and couldn't understand why he had done this
to me.

"Why did you do that?" I demanded. "Why did you
want to hurt me?"

The boy didn't answer, and when I saw the tears begin
to well up in his eyes I gave him a disdainful shove and he
ran off.

My sister and cousin had run home when I grabbed the
boy, so I finally rounded up the horse and led him back to
my grandfather's house. The welcome was not the con-
quering hero's welcome I had expected. The news had
preceded me, and my aunt and grandparents were very
perturbed because I had laid hands on a white boy, as
this is something that just wasn't done in Mississippi, regardless of the provocation, you understand.

"Archie Lee," my auntie scolded, "I want you to promise me that you'll never hit a white person again."

"No," I stubbornly refused. "That boy did wrong and
deserved to be punished whether he was black or white."

Auntie tried to reason with me. She pleaded, cajoled, threatened. But I was firm. I would not back down. I felt that I was right, and I had not yet learned to fear the white man's retribution in those days. I just could not understand why I should be discriminated against because of the color of my skin. Right was right, and wrong was wrong, and if a person did a bad thing he should be punished regardless of his color.

My auntie finally gave up and said that we would have to return to St. Louis because my presence in Mississippi would only cause trouble for our relatives. And so, I had my first taste of social inequity and discrimination.

Another incident that made a deep impression on me occurred in my boyhood days in St. Louis when an excessively fat lady passed our house as my auntie and I were sitting on the front porch.

"Poor lady," Auntie remarked. "She's headed right for the graveyard."

"Why?" I asked.

"All that fat is just too much for her heart," Auntie replied. Then, realizing that I needed a clearer explanation, she said, "It's like the farmer who had a small farm and had a small pump to irrigate the farm. Well, as the farmer prospered, he bought more land, and he kept on buying more and more land as time went on."

I was confused. "Well, wasn't that smart?" I asked.

"Yes, that part was smart. But he tried to irrigate this greater amount of land with the same small pump, and it was just too much for that little pump to handle, so eventually the pump broke down and there was no water for the land, so it just died."

This was an explanation I could understand, and it was a lesson that remained with me through my boxing days.

When I tended to get too heavy I remembered the story about the overworked pump and acted accordingly.

St. Louis was now my home. My mother married Mordell Brown, and Auntie wanted me to know my mother and stepfather, so she sent me and Rachel to visit them on weekends. I was fascinated by my stepfather, who, like my uncle, was a hardworking man as well as a veteran of World War I. I never tired of hearing his stories about the war.

My mother gave birth to another son, Samuel, and soon after this, Mordell Brown died and Samuel was taken in by Auntie.

We all used to share in doing the chores, and one of these chores was bringing in the wood from the woodshed in back of the house. I was pretty mischievous, and I used to tell Sammy about the demons that hid in the woodpile, and the demons that hid in his bedroom, and that unless I was with him to protect him, he was in big trouble. And, of course, I warned him about the especially terrible demon that even I couldn't protect him from that would get him if he ever told Auntie what I had told him about the "demons."

Eventually, my mother married again and gave birth to another son, Louis, and he was really smart. In fact, he was the smartest of us all. He learned things very easily, I think a little too easily, because he got so that he wouldn't do anything unless it could be done in an easy way. For example, he found that he could win marbles easier from his friends by shooting craps for them rather than developing the skill necessary to win them legitimately, and he soon had more marbles than he knew what to do with. And he found another way to take his friends' marbles away. He became a marble loan shark, loaning out ten marbles and getting fifteen back in return. He was pretty sharp.

The first school I went to was the Dumas School, an all-black school—not because of official segregation, you understand, but because of its location in an all-black section. My fondest memory of this school was the fact that it was situated near the Loose-Wiles Biscuit Company, and for a nickel I could buy a bag full of broken but delicious cookies.

My sister, my stepbrother and I were trained to help with the work around the house: washing dishes, making beds, bringing in wood and other chores, and I really enjoyed the responsibility of doing these things. When we moved to Biddle Street I went to the Jefferson School. I liked school and learned easily. I had my share of fights as a boy, and the first I recall was with a boy named Johnny Cunningham. I lost a tooth in that fracas. Another incident I remember vividly is the day my sister and I were walking home from school with my closest friend, Mose Howell, and Mose's brother Reuben. My sister teased Reuben to the point where he finally slapped her, which infuriated me. The fact that Reuben was four years older than me, and much bigger and heavier, did not stop me from coming to Rachel's aid. I held Reuben even in the fight, and when it was over I was proud of having defended my sister and holding my own with the bigger boy.

As many boys do, I once ran away from home for a fancied wrong done me. My stepbrother Sammy had been kept after school, so I was told to take over Sammy's chores, which I thought was unfair. So I rebelled, as youngsters are wont to do, and took a few of my belongings and some food that Auntie had prepared for that evening's meal and took off through the backyard to a

used-car lot just in back of the house. I crawled into the
back seat of an old sedan, and as I laid there I thought
how my auntie and uncle would miss me and how they
would be sorry about what they had done, and I had vi-
sions of them begging me to come back. As the afternoon
wore on and it became dark, I was getting cold and
cramped in my tiny refuge, and I became increasingly
miserable as the glamour of being a runaway wore off and
I thought of my auntie and uncle relaxing and reading,
and Rachel and Sammy playing in the comfortable,
homey warmth of the house. Finally, I could stand it no
more, so I returned to the house, where Auntie was waiting for me.

"Archie Lee," she said sternly, "you go right on up to
your room. I saw you get into that old car pretending to
run away, and you can run away anytime you want, but
the next time you do, don't steal the food I made for sup-
per. That's what I'm going to spank you for—stealing
food—not for running away." And so I learned another
valuable lesson from my auntie.

The next school I went to was the Lincoln School,
which was a combination junior-high and high school and
was a school for blacks. It was a nice school, new and
clean, built in 1927. I weighed 110 pounds at the time
and was too small for football, but I was very strong and
liked to box. A fighter by the name of Kid Roberts lived
in my neighborhood, and Roberts had a brother named
Bat Grant, whom he had taught the rudiments of boxing.
Bat needed someone to spar with, so he taught me. We
sparred many rounds together while Kid Roberts
watched and instructed both of us. Kid Roberts felt that I
showed good potential and encouraged me. Emboldened
by this I became involved in many fights, of which I won
some and lost some.

I became a juvenile delinquent in spite of Auntie's teachings and my regular attendance at a Baptist church and Sunday school. When I am asked how I managed to change from a delinquent to a law-abiding citizen, I simply reply, "I grew up." Which is the way it happened, you understand.

In my delinquency days I belonged to a gang, as did practically every other boy in that area. The gangs were divided into different groups. The Irish, the Jews, the blacks and the Italians all had their own gangs, and we fought, but with fists mostly, and occasionally with rocks, and there was very little of the extremely violent type of gang-fighting which in later days involved the use of knives, guns, chains and other weapons that so often resulted in serious injuries or even deaths. Among our gangs, many times a dispute was settled by each gang choosing their best man and having these two fight it out. After it was over there would be handshaking all around and peace would be restored—at least for a while. In those days the youths also had more respect for adult and police authority. A single adult could break up a gang fight, and talking back to or assaulting a police officer was unthinkable.

My sister and I were quite close—walking to school together, exchanging confidences—and a good brother-sister relationship existed between us. However, as we grew older, I noticed that we were gradually drifting apart as she became interested in a young man by the name of Elihu Williams. At the same time I had two pals, Robert Stamps and Eddie Williams, and we all shared a common interest in boxing.

Rachel soon married Elihu Williams and rented an apartment in a nice neighborhood, and I enjoyed visiting her often. She would make cake and other delicacies for me, and we enjoyed talking about our life with our beloved auntie and uncle. I always dreamed about becoming an uncle myself, because I thought uncles were just the greatest. Unfortunately, Uncle Cleveland died shortly after Rachel got married. It happened while he was being initiated into a fraternal organization. During the hazing an accident occurred, leaving him paralyzed, and he soon died. On his deathbed, Uncle Cleveland called me in and asked me to promise to take care of my auntie, a promise I gladly gave and always did my best to fulfill.

Soon after this, Rachel gave birth to twins, but she died in childbirth. One of the twins, a boy, lived four months, and the girl, June, survived and was taken in by Auntie. Uncle Cleveland had left Auntie with what was considered quite a bit of money in those days. She received $3,500 from an insurance policy and $800 in benefits from two fraternal organizations. However, she was not experienced in handling money. Being soft-hearted, she helped relatives and friends who needed money, and it kept going out with nothing coming in, so before long the money was gone. This being during the Depression, we were soon on welfare, as were most of our neighbors.

TWELVE

•

After the death of my uncle I kind of went wild and turned to petty thievery because I wanted money to do various things. Although boxing for a career was always in the back of my mind, I didn't think of it seriously at this time. I wanted to buy a trumpet and become a musician, but Auntie refused to buy me one, as she had once read about the death of a famous trumpet player whose obituary stated that he had blown his lungs out. And she took this literally, so she ruled out my becoming a trumpet player. She had a piano in the house, which she had acquired in better days, and offered to have me take piano lessons, but I wanted to be either a trumpet or saxophone player, so I stole in the hope of saving enough money to buy a trumpet, but I could never save anything. Knowing Auntie would never agree to getting me the trumpet, I decided to ask my schoolteacher to help me, but somehow when I spoke to her, instead of asking for a trumpet, I asked for boxing gloves. I don't place any significant interpretation on this switch as to my future destiny, but I feel that I made the switch because a trumpet would have been too expensive, you understand, and my teacher knew of my interest in boxing. Also, I thought she might laugh at the idea of me becoming a musician. Besides, in the back of my mind, I thought that perhaps after she agreed to buy the boxing gloves for me, maybe I could step up my promotion to the desired trumpet. My teacher suggested that I shop around in the pawnshops and find a pair at a good price, and she also asked me to keep my eye out for a lamp for her. So I stole two oil lamps from my house and sold them to my teacher for two dollars, and with the money I bought my first boxing gloves.

Along with the rest of my gang, I began pilfering more and more, stealing lead pipes and copper wiring out of empty houses. We reasoned that stealing was a matter of survival—a way of life in tough Depression times. I knew that eventually I would be caught, but the desire to have a little spending money forced me to overlook this. I was caught three times. The third time was for stealing money from a streetcar. My friend Arthur Knox would pull down the pole from which the streetcar received its electrical power from an overhead powerline, stopping the street-car. When the motorman got out to replace the pole, I would dash onto the streetcar and steal the change from his cash box. I was sentenced to three years in the Mis-souri Training School at Booneville and was paroled after serving twenty-two months. I have already described what life was like during that miserable period of my life, so I won't go into that any further. In fact, I'd like to for-get that whole experience. But an experience it was, and at least I learned something from it and turned it to my benefit in the long run. As a condition of my parole, I had to get a job, and my mother was instrumental in helping me through my parole officer and a playground superin-tendent by the name of Thomas Brooks, now a police captain, who got me a job with an ice and coal dealer. My job was to stand on the step of an old Model-T pickup truck shouting, "Coal, wood for sale." It was freezing cold and I had no overcoat, while the owner-driver of the truck was snugly enthroned in the closed cab, wearing a warm overcoat and with a bucket of glowing coals at his feet for additional warmth. At each stop I would fill a tub with coal that weighed in the neighborhood of eighty pounds and run this load to the customer, who many times lived in a third-floor apartment. I worked twelve hours that first day and had been promised a dollar for my day's work. When we got back to the coal dealer's basement "office" at the end of the day, however, the man gave me a half-dollar instead. He said that business had been bad and he couldn't afford to pay a dollar. I was furious, especially because he was taking advantage of me, knowing that I had to keep working as a condition of my parole. I think that this was the only time in my life that I felt capable of killing another man. There were icepicks stuck in the wall, and I felt that I wanted to jerk them from the wall and plunge them into him time and again, but I held myself back and just threw the half-dollar back at the man and told him if he needed money that bad he could keep it.

Fortunately, my parole officer sided with me when he heard of the circumstances and suggested that I look for something to do on my own. When I told my auntie the story, she told me that she was proud of me for holding my temper, and that the experience I had gained that day was worth much more than the dollar I had lost.

However, I was still faced with the problem of getting a job or going back to reform school. One day I happened to pass my friend Arthur James' house and I thought I would go in and say hello to his mother. James was still in reform school. He was another who, like me, vowed to make something of himself and never go back. Mrs.

James gave me a piece of cake and a glass of milk and was happy to learn of her son's vow to stay out of trouble in the future. She was well off financially in comparison with the rest of the community. She worked for the Liggett & Myers Tobacco Company, and she owned her own home, where she boarded some of her fellow workers. I asked Mrs. James if she could get me a job at the plant, but she shook her head sadly and said that due to the times people were being laid off. She offered me a job as her housekeeper, however, which I willingly accepted. I worked washing dishes, making beds and scrubbing floors while the boarders were away at work, and then on Wednesdays and Saturdays, when Mrs. James was not working, she would supervise my handling of other household chores. I was paid $3 a week for my work, and there were many fringe benefits—such as free meals. Mrs. James was continually buying things for her son for the day when he would return home, and at the same time she would buy a similar item for me, whom she regarded as her son while her own was away. And so, in return, I reciprocated by doing extra chores to show my appreciation. Arthur James, like me, kept his word to make something of himself and became successful and well-respected.

THIRTEEN

●

I was eighteen years old when I was released from reform school and was, in the eyes of matchmakers and fight managers, inexperienced as a fighter. At this time the Civilian Conservation Corps was organized as an emergency measure to help boys who were having difficulty finding work in those hard times. It got boys off the streets and was a great juvenile-delinquency deterrent. It was government-supervised and was outside work, and I felt that this was ideal for me, as I would not only be able to send my auntie some money, but would be able to improve myself physically. My parole officer agreed to allow me to join the C.C.C., and I became a member of Camp 3760 at Poplar Bluff, Missouri. I earned $30 a month, of which $25 was sent home, leaving me $5 a month for my own needs.

The camp at Poplar Bluff was new and clean, so new that our army cots hadn't arrived, so we were forced to sleep on the floor temporarily. I didn't mind, as this seemed like heaven after reform-school life. I was in the forestry division, and our job was to clear out roads for the engineers and surveyors. It was hard work, but it was the kind of work I wanted to toughen up my body for my intended boxing career. With this in mind I worked very hard, harder than most of the other boys, who thought I must be out of my mind to go at the pace I had set for myself. We would go to work in a large stake truck with our equipment piled in with us, and the boys would sit on the bed of the truck, talking, telling jokes and singing, but I stationed myself behind the cab of the truck, standing upright, and as the branches of trees would lash out over the top of the cab, I would wait until the last fraction of a second and then bob and weave and duck out of the way. It was a dangerous game, for if I failed to duck in time a heavy branch could have split my head open. But it was good training, and was a technique that helped me many times in the ring, for through this I developed my ring style.

Captain Ralph Parks, who was in charge of the camp, was a sports enthusiast, and when I asked permission to organize a boxing team he readily agreed. He agreed not only because of his love of sports, but because he also felt that outside activity was good for the morale and was an outlet for the great drive and restlessness inherent in most youths. The camp also had a basketball team, a swimming team and an orchestra to keep the boys busy and out of trouble.

Quite a few boys became interested in joining my boxing team, and I taught them to box, and in teaching them I also learned and developed my own skill further. I beat all comers, and in 1936 our team entered the Golden Gloves, and all my teammates with one exception won their bouts over the Southeastern and Missouri and Illinois boxers. I won too, but was beaten in the finals in St. Louis by Courtland Schultz. However, I later won the tri-state sectional tournament, and my team also made a very good showing in this tournament.

One fight that left a deep impression on me was with a

local boy from a nearby town whose brother happened to
be the referee. Claiming his brother had been fouled in
the first round, the referee stopped the fight for a while to
give his brother time to recover from the terrific beating
he had been taking, but when the fight resumed I proceeded to knock the boy out. The home-town crowd
made derogatory racial remarks and became hostile and
Captain Parks wanted to avoid trouble, so he ordered us
to hurry to the trucks and had us take the governors off so
that we could go faster. I didn't even have time to get out
of my ring gear. The trucks raced to the camp, followed
closely by a large group of the town's people in a caval-
cade of cars.

When we got to camp, Captain Parks ordered a spotlight played on the entrance to the camp and stood there
with a submachine gun, and when the belligerent town
bullies got out of their cars he warned them that they
were on government property and that he would do everything in his power to defend it. The sight of the submachine gun and Captain Parks' stern warning cooled
the mob down. After a bit of grumbling they returned to
town.

A fight early in my career that still stands out strongly
in my mind occurred when I was still in the C.C.C. An
up-and-coming fighter by the name of Alan Mathews was
training at our camp for a fight with Benny Deathpane,
which was to be held at the stadium at Poplar Bluff. Captain Parks gave permission to the boys who wanted to see
the fight to use the camp trucks. We were very excited
about getting to see this fight.

In the preliminary, Billy Simms, a light-heavyweight,
fought another boxer who would not put up a fight, and
the crowd booed while Simms, a local fighter, tried to explain that it wasn't his fault, that the other boy just

Archie and Rocky Marciano sign for their heavyweight title fight in New York in 1955. Archie knocked Rocky down in the second round, but the heavyweight champion came back and won with a knockout in the ninth.

Archie talks to a group of youngsters in a St. Louis, Missouri, youth center in 1967. He was a consultant with the Office of Economic Opportunity and was traveling across the country talking with boys. (UPI)

(*Above and opposite*) Archie with some of his boys from the ABC Club in San Diego, California. (UPI)

Archie watches Julio Neves go down and out in the third round of their fight in Rio de Janeiro in 1958. (UPI)

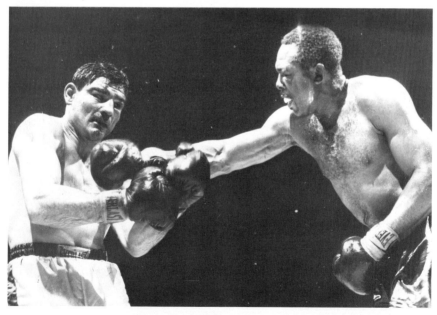

Giulio Rinaldi takes a long right from Archie during their fifteen-round title fight in New York City in 1961. Archie won a decision as fight went the limit. This was one of Archie's last fights. (UPI)

Yolande Pompey hits the deck for the third time in the tenth round during their championship fight in London in 1956.

Learning from the old master.   (UPI)

Archie having a heart-to-heart talk with a prospective ABC member.

Some of the ABC boys being treated to ice cream.

Archie working the speed bag.

Archie lecturing at Los Amigos High School in Garden Grove, California. Youngest son, Anthony, is with him.

wouldn't fight. The boys from the C.C.C. shouted that
they had somebody who would fight, indicating me, and
the crowd took up the demand. I didn't have any equipment with me, but the management, not wanting a riot
on their hands, obtained an old pair of swimming trunks
and some sneakers for me. I fought without any foul protection, and a blow below the belt could have been disastrous, but, encouraged by the enthusiasm of my friends, I
proceeded to give Simms a thorough beating before
knocking him out.

I then dressed and came back in time to watch the
bout between Deathpane and Mathews. In the fifth
round, Mathews knocked Deathpane out with a vicious,
solid hook to the body, and the crowd again booed because they didn't realize that a shot like Deathpane had
received could knock a man out just as easily as one to
the jaw. The crowd demanded that Mathews fight me,
but although I said nothing, I hoped that I wouldn't have
to, because I knew I was no match for the older, more experienced Mathews. George Wilsman, Mathews' manager, also knew that we didn't belong in the same ring, so
he would not okay the match. However, I was regarded
as quite a hero by my buddies after my knockout of
Simms.

Shortly after this, I had an experience that nearly cost
me my life and left an emotional scar that I carry to this
day. A group of us C.C.C. boys had a little time off and
wanted to visit friends and relatives in St. Louis, but we
had no money and decided we would hop a freight train.
The train turned out to be a slow one, stopping at every
whistle stop along the way, but I didn't mind—at least it
was free. I was riding on a tank car containing molasses,
holding on to the rail running around the car with one
hand while in the other I clutched a bag containing my

ring equipment, as I thought I might possibly be able to get a fight in St. Louis. Suddenly I saw the boys in the front of me run to the next car and climb the ladder to the top. Instinctively I whirled around and saw a brakeman, red-faced with rage, rushing at me with a club raised over his head. As the man swung the club with devastating force, I weaved slightly and the club smashed to pieces against the side of the car. If this terrific blow had struck me I was certain that my skull would have been crushed and my brains splattered on the side of that freight car. I dropped my bag as I fell straddling the catwalk, my foot hitting the spinning wheel, but I quickly got up, scrambled up the ladder and ran across the tops of several boxcars before I caught up with my friends. The brakeman, without the benefit of his club, did not pursue. I have never been able to figure out why a man, especially in Depression times, would try to murder a boy merely because he was trying to get a ride he could not afford to pay for. The free ride would not have cost the brakeman, the railroad or anyone else anything, and I couldn't figure out why the brakeman acted as he did.

Later, a good Samaritan found the bag containing my ring equipment and took the trouble to look me up and return it. For this I was grateful, not so much for the material value of the returned equipment, but because it helped to restore my faith in people after my narrow escape from death. The look on that brakeman's face as he came at me with that club—the soul-baring viciousness and hatred on his snarling, anger-twisted features, was something that was to haunt me for many years to come. It was something I had never seen before, even among the guards at the reform school. It was something I didn't even know existed, but I was to see this same look of the devil on people's faces again, unfortunately. I saw it on the faces of Hitler and his Nazis as they brutally beat, tortured and killed 6 million Jews. And I saw this again when I recently saw a movie on the life of the great advocate of nonviolence, that great American, Martin Luther King. Here were these blacks, just trying to get the things guaranteed them by the Constitution—the right to vote, the right to life, liberty and the pursuit of happiness—and these brutal policemen would shove a nightstick ten inches into a woman's belly, or crack somebody's skull open, just because they were asking for something that belonged to them. And it wasn't just the skull-breaking and the beatings, it was that look again on the faces of those men—the same viciousness and hatred and anger and brutality along with a look of pleasurable anticipation that I had seen on that brakeman's face. And I saw it again in Chicago as firemen used high-pressure hoses on little boys and girls, sending them skidding down the street, breaking bones and picking up ugly bruises as they were swept along.

I guess that trip to St. Louis was one I just never should have made. Not only did I come close to losing my life, but the return trip was also a bad scene. I left St. Louis Sunday evening, and this time at least I was smart enough to catch a manifest train, which goes faster and has fewer stops, as it carries perishable goods. But even so, I arrived back in Poplar Bluff at midnight, just in time to see the lights of the camp truck disappearing in the distance, and my heart sunk down to my stomach for a minute, but then I realized that the only way I was going to get back to camp was to start out by shank's mare, so I started walking the fifteen miles back to the camp. I had to be back before the morning bugle sounded, so I cast superstition aside and decided to take a shortcut through a graveyard.

It was a little scary, walking alone through that ebony-black graveyard with the white monuments, because with a little imagination one could see a white monument materialize—or maybe it would be better to say dematerialize—and look like a wispy ghost. But I wasn't bothered too much, because I knew deep down that the dead couldn't do you any harm. It was the living who did the damage.

Well, anyway, I came out of the cemetery without any problems, but as I left and was walking down a gravel road, I heard footsteps behind me, and they were keeping time with the crunching of my shoes on the gravel. If I stopped, the footsteps behind me also stopped, and if I slowed down, the footsteps also slowed down, and when I speeded up, the footsteps speeded up. It was pitch black and I could feel my heart kind of racing. It was getting kind of spooky. I didn't know what else to do, so I just kept on walking as if everything was okay. I reasoned that there was no use panicking, so I just kept on going, although I'll admit that my pace did pick up a bit, but no matter how fast I walked, the footsteps behind me seemed to be gaining on me. I turned my head, but could see nothing in the inky blackness, and I began to wonder if there really was such a thing as ghosts. But I had always heard that ghosts travel soundlessly; that the only noises they make are vocal, such as wails and sighs and screams, so if this was a ghost, he wasn't following accepted ghostly practice.

Suddenly there was a light right alongside me and I saw a man's face as he lit a cigarette and let out a diabolical laugh, sending a chill racing up my spine. I never did find out what or who it was, and I was never too interested in finding out, because I might not have liked the answer. But I still feel that chill racing up my spine whenever I think of this incident.

I walked all through that night, stopping only a few minutes occasionally to rest. A few cars passed, but nobody would stop to give me a lift, and I made it into camp with a little to spare, but I was tired, and one of my buddies covered me with leaves so I could grab a few winks on the job that day.

Discipline in the C.C.C. was very much like the discipline in the army, and on satisfactory completion of our time in the C.C.C. we would get honorable discharges. I wasn't sure what good or harm having or not having the honorable discharge would do, but I didn't want to take any chances, as I already had a couple of strikes against me. Maybe it would be a good job reference, so I decided that I wanted that honorable discharge when I got out. But I almost didn't make it, because of a big rebellion we had one time. What it was all about, you see, we all were entitled to three hot meals a day, but as we would get deeper and deeper in the woods our noon meals would become colder and colder, and certain things like cold soup or stew really weren't the best-tasting things. But our supervisor paid no attention to our complaints. Then a boy named Sam said he would not work unless he could get the hot meals he was supposed to get. So our supervisor decided to bring things to a head and told all those who felt like Sam did to line up on one side of the road and those who were satisfied to line up on the other. All of the boys but one joined Sam. This exception was a huge hulk of a guy, but he spoke, strangely enough, in an effeminate voice. Anyway, he just sat there on the other side, and I felt that he was insulting us by not joining us, so I walked across the road and told him to get his tail on over to our side of the road and make it unanimous or I was going to let him have it. Well, he just sat there without blinking an eye or answering, so I let him have my Sunday punch right on the jaw. Then he blinked his eyes and the tears started coming, and he asked plaintively, "Why you do that?"

Well, let me tell you, that guy must have had a granite jaw, because I felt pain all the way from my knuckles to my shoulder. If he would have come at me, about the only thing I could have done was run, because that arm was absolutely useless. But I thought I would try to pull a bluff first and acted like I was all right, but I guess he didn't notice that the fist I threatened him with this time was my left, and that my right arm was just hanging at my side, too numb to lift. And so I waved my left fist close to his nose and said, "Maybe that will teach you to stick with your buddies. Now, get your tail over there before I smack you again."

So he meekly crossed over and joined us against the supervisor, who had us pile in the trucks and head back to camp to let Captain Parks settle the matter. Captain Parks called a meeting and raised a lot of sand, and he picked out the strike's organizers and told them that they would have to leave the camp that very day and that they would get dishonorable discharges. Luckily, my part in this affair wasn't mentioned. I think this was due to the benefits I had brought the camp through my boxing program.

Another incident that I got involved in was when a new kid joined us by the name of Harry Chitwood. Well, Harry didn't feel that the rules and common courtesies were made for him, so instead of falling in at the end of a line he would break into the head of the line. And in the mess hall he would grab food away from guys, although there was plenty for everybody. He felt that nobody had a right to tell him what to do, and he made himself generally obnoxious. So I decided to give him a lesson in manners, and since he wouldn't listen to reason I waited for him after mess one day and gave him a mild going-over. He, of course, went to Captain Parks about the incident, and Captain Parks fined me $2 of my monthly $5 and made me keep my hands in my pockets for two weeks when I wasn't eating or working. This wasn't easy to do, but I wanted that honorable discharge, so I did as I was told. I used to hear from Harry Chitwood every so often since that affair, and we would laugh over it.

While I was in the C.C.C. I was fighting in every tournament I could, representing the camp, and I was doing real well. Toward the end of my service in the C.C.C., Billy Ciscoe became interested in me and told me that he could get me a fight over the weekend and that I would get $10 for the bout, which was in Hot Springs, Arkansas. I agreed and fought the Pocohantas Kid and knocked him out in the second round. However, instead of the $10 I had been promised, I received only $3, as Ciscoe explained that $7 had been deducted for expenses.

I eventually left the C.C.C. with an honorable discharge and went back to St. Louis, where I got a federal part-time job that paid $19 a month. In a short time I switched to the Works Progress Administration, another government-sponsored organization intended to help the poverty-stricken. On this job I received $22 a week, $14 of which was in cash and the balance in food and sometimes clothing. I continued all the while to do roadwork and train to keep in condition for my prospective boxing career.

I became good friends with George Porter, a bantamweight, who introduced me to Monroe Harrison, and

Harrison took me and Porter to see the Kessler brothers, Harry, Benny and Solly, who were fight promoters. Harry Kessler later became a referee and was the referee in my title fight with Rocky Marciano. Benny Kessler promoted a fight between me and A.A.U. Champion Julius Kemp, a top-rated amateur in the welterweight division, and I won by a knockout in the third round at the West Side Ball Park in St. Louis.

I then met a manager named Kid Bandy and sparred with Bandy's fighter, Joey Parks, who was a clever boxer. Bandy got me a fight with Speedy Schaeffer in Quincy, Illinois, and we fought to a draw. Next, Bandy secured a spot for me on an entertainment card, which was a combination of vaudeville acts, boxing and wrestling, and more of an exhibition than a regular bout, and my opponent was Charley Dawson. For this exhibition I received $3, but when the A.A.U. heard about it they revoked my amateur license, so I then turned professional.

I was still working on the W.P.A., and most of my small earnings went to help support my auntie and my family. One extremely cold day our crew was working outside and we built a fire in an old trash can to keep warm. Our boss came by and told us to put the fire out, but we refused. The boss then told us that unless we put the fire out he would discharge us, which meant disaster, because jobs in those days just were not to be found. However, we still refused, and the boss kicked the fire out himself. This demonstration of man's inhumanity to man made me angry, so I quit, deciding that I would devote full-time to becoming a professional boxer.

Soon after this my friend Monroe Harrison coached me in the style of fighting that I improvised on and developed. I call this the shell technique, and it consists of keeping both hands cocked in front, which not only affords an excellent defense, but also permits a fighter to hit very rapidly and without warning with either hand. The first time I used this technique was in a tournament in Cleveland and my opponent was Frankie Nelson, a very aggressive fighter who was continually throwing punches. The shell technique worked well defensively, but I was kept so busy defending myself that I had very little chance to go on the offensive. I lacked the experience to use this technique offensively, especially against a fighter of Nelson's style. The referee stopped the fight, thinking that I was hurt, but a sportswriter felt that I had quit and wrote this in his column. It took me a long time to live this down.

My next manager was George Wilsman, who took me to Ponca City, Oklahoma, for a fight. I had been promised $35 for this fight, but received only $12.

A short time later I met a man named Cal Thompson, who came to my dressing room after one of my fights. He was a real sharp dresser and a very persuasive talker. "Archie," he told me, "you've got a lot of class. You've got it, man."

"Well, thanks, Mr. Thompson," I said. My ears had perked up at the praise of this man, who impressed me by his expensive clothes and smooth talk.

"Yes, Archie," he went on, "you've got it. But, you know, in this game just having it isn't enough. You've got to have a good manager who can bring you along right, pace you just right, get you in the right fights."

I nodded my head. "I couldn't agree with you more," I told him.

"How many fights have you had, Archie?"

"Well," I said, "professionally only seven, but I've had

a lot of fights and a good record as an amateur." I went
on to tell him about all those kayos I had placed upon
guys as an amateur.

Thompson seemed surprised. "You sure look like a man
who's been a pro longer than that," he said.

In one sense he was praising me, but in another sense it
was a put-down, probably to make the proposition he was
about to offer more acceptable.

"Look," he said, "you come with me. Let me manage
you and I'll get you all the fights you want. I'll make you
the champion of the world."

Well, those are the kind of words I wanted to hear, you
know, and I thought, well, this must be a terrific guy, and
he'll get me somewhere in a hurry, and this plus the fact
that I hadn't had a fight in almost four months decided
me right then and there that I wanted this guy to handle
me. He was telling me all these good things, you know,
and anyone who has ever been to a fortune-teller knows
that this is just how they operate. They tell you all kind of
good things—like you are going to become rich, or make
a trip, or get a promotion and all this sort of thing. Well,
the mind is funny, because if just one of these predictions
comes true you remember it and think, well, this fortune-
teller is great. You forget all about the things she told you
that didn't come true. So, anyway, I said, "Mr. Thompson, I would like you to manage me. When do we start?"

Thompson was all smiles. "Right now," he said as he
shook my hand. "Right now. And believe me, Archie,
you're going places."

His look of success really convinced me, and I had vi-
sions of being a champion in a very short time, and of the
money rolling in. Now I could really help my mother and
my auntie and our family, and I could help kids, and I
could find some nice girl and get married and have kids of

my own. And so Cal Thompson became my manager. His promises to make my dreams of fame and wealth come true completely won me over, and George Wilsman became my ex-manager. I didn't have any contract with him, so there was nothing he could hold me to; and, besides, he had gotten me so few fights recently that I felt that I owed him nothing. Being under the legal age to sign a contract, I had only a verbal agreement with Thompson, which was not binding, as I was a minor. If he couldn't live up to his lavish promises I was under no obligation to stay with him. But I didn't think that I would ever leave him. He had me so completely convinced that he could take me to the championship of the world that I was way up in the clouds. I came down to earth as I heard Thompson say, "Look, Archie, now that this thing is agreed, why don't you come and move into my house. We could save on expenses. I've got plenty of room."

"Fine with me," I replied. My mother was living with us now and was supporting the family, who had high hopes that before too long my fistic career would start paying off so I could help out. But in the meantime, having one less mouth to feed would be a big help, especially when it was my mouth, as I liked to eat.

And so we drove to Thompson's house in his new, shiny black 1937 Dodge, a beautiful car with whitewall tires and two gleaming chrome spotlights. This man had class with a capital C. And I was further impressed when we arrived at his house.

"Well, here it is," he said. "My humble abode."

The house was far from being a "humble abode," and when we went inside I saw a big piano in the beautiful and large living room, and there were three bedrooms, a dining room, a kitchen and *two* bathrooms. And everything was so tastefully and elegantly furnished. I told myself that this was one of the things I wanted sometime—a beautiful home—and I would install a beautiful wife in it and we would have lots of beautiful children.

I guess my eyes were pretty big as I took in all these things and Thompson laughed. He was enjoying showing off his house, and he was rightfully proud of it, as this was one of the status symbols, along with his fine car, that showed the world that he had made his mark.

"Let's have a sandwich," he said.

"Fine," I agreed. He knew how to cement a relationship with an always hungry Archie Moore. We went to the spotless kitchen and made some bologna-and-cheese sandwiches and drank some milk while we talked about future plans.

I wasn't to stay in Cal Thompson's house too long, however. The morning after I arrived, I watched as Mrs. Thompson made toast in the toaster, and this really intrigued me. I had never seen toast made that way before, as Auntie had always made toast on the stove after buttering the bread, of course. So after the kids went off to school and Cal went down to open up his barber shop and Mrs. Thompson left for her dress shop, I proceeded to make toast on the fascinating toaster. Of course, I did it the way Auntie did it—I buttered the toast before putting it in the toaster—and I ate a whole loaf of bread. But the butter I had put on the bread before I put it in the toaster ruined that piece of equipment, and Mrs. Thompson was quite unhappy about that, for which I don't blame her, you understand. So Mrs. Thompson wanted me out of there, and what really finally persuaded Thompson to pay attention to his wife's wishes was my habit of getting up early in the morning to do roadwork. I would get up hours before anybody else in the house, and when I went into the kitchen to make breakfast the noise

I made bothered the other people, who were still sleeping. So Thompson soon had me out of there and had me stay at a boarding house nearby, which I didn't mind, as the food was great.

I had seven fights in nine months, and I had a girlfriend by the name of Gladys Walker, and I was feeling pretty good. At first Gladys wasn't too friendly, but after I started coming on with an impressive string of wins, her attitude changed. It didn't cost me much to take her out, as neither of us smoked or drank, and for a couple of bucks we could go out and have a fine time.

Thompson got me a wonderful trainer by the name of Hiawatha Grey, who I have used off and on throughout the years. At that time I still had a lot of rough edges and he smoothed them out, and even more important he curbed my impatience and made me think and act like a professional fighter instead of an anxious, hungry kid who wanted to make a name for himself in a hurry. Many a fighter has been ruined by a manager who brought him up in class too fast. What most people don't understand about the fight game is that there really are different divisions, you know, in regard to class—or rather, I should say *ability* of a fighter. It's just like in baseball, where there are major leagues and minor leagues, and a minor-league team just doesn't have a chance against a major-league team. Well, it's the same in boxing, and usually, all other things being equal—such as guts, condition and natural ability—it's experience in the ring that carries a fighter on to the top. But it's very dangerous to him and his career if he is still a minor-leaguer and tries to suddenly jump up into the major league. He can suffer a setback that he will never get over mentally, physically and prestige-wise, you see. I was treading on dangerous ground trying to hurry things too fast. That ground could turn into quicksand. Patience is something Hiawatha Grey taught me, among other things.

And yet, I felt that Thompson was bringing me along *too* slow, and I didn't want to wait until I was an old man before becoming a champion, which I had to do anyway as it turned out, but that's another story. Anyway, I had 12 fights in 1937 and 1 up to that time in 1938, and had won all 13 fights, 11 of them by knockouts, and I felt that it was about time that I moved up in class, and that maybe a move to another area would be good. In 1937 I had beaten Charley Dawson for the Kansas middleweight title, Dynamite Payne for the Oklahoma middleweight title, and Deacon Logan for the Missouri middleweight championship, so you see, it wasn't just that I was being impatient. I felt that I was ready.

FOURTEEN

•

About that time two things happened that really gave me the impetus to make a move to what I felt would be greener pastures in order to get ahead in this fistic business: My romance with Gladys cooled off, and I met a man named Felix Thurman.

Felix was a top-notch mechanic and owned a small garage. He knew absolutely nothing about managing a fighter, but I liked Felix for his honesty and his sincere desire to see me get somewhere in the fight game. He had faith and confidence in my ability and suggested that we go to California, where he had heard that boxing was very popular and that there were good opportunities for a young boxer. It sounded solid, like great adventure, and I was getting to the point where I felt that I needed a change of scenery. George Porter kept telling me about how I wouldn't have a chance out on the West Coast. That guys like Johnny "The Bandit" Romero would absolutely kill me, but the more George needled me the more I wanted to go west and make him eat his words. So I told Felix that I would go with him, and he sold his garage, keeping only his expensive tools, which we took along with us. And they came in handy in more ways than one. Not only did they keep our old car running, but we later had to sell them to keep in food and gas. The provisions we stocked with for the trip were soft drinks, apples and peanuts, plus thirty-odd dollars. Talk about faith! We had more than our share.

Things went pretty smooth until March 30, 1938, when we were passing through Oklahoma. It was kind of a cold, damp, overcast day, and the gloomy weather was a sign of what was to come. We were going down this road when I saw a car coming in our direction, and it was trying to pass the car in front of him. He got in our lane, barreling along at a pretty good clip, and I could see that he was never going to make it back to his own lane before crashing head-on into us. I felt the skin crawling on the back of my neck, and my stomach went into a knot, and instinctively I hollered, "Look out!" to Felix and made a lunge for the wheel, but he was just as aware of the situation as I was, and he threw an elbow up to keep me from grabbing the wheel and just before the oncoming car crashed into us, at the last split second, waiting until there was nothing else he could do, Felix swung the wheel over, taking the car off the road. There was grass on the shoulder we hit, and it was soft and wet and flipped the car over and knocked both of us unconscious. I noticed afterward that the driver of the car that had caused us to go off the road paid us no mind; he just kept going on his merry way, not caring if we were hurt or killed or that we had probably saved his life as well as ours by going onto that shoulder.

When I came to I heard a dripping sound, which I thought was gasoline. I looked over at Felix, and he was still out, kind of crumpled up like, and I shook him a little, trying to bring him to, and I yelled, "Hey, Felix, come on! Wake up! We got to get out of here!" But Felix didn't move. He just kind of groaned a little, so I figured it was up to me before the whole thing went up in flames because of that leaking gas. I fought desperately to get out of the car, but the door was jammed, and we were upside-down. I wasn't getting anywhere. I tried to kick the window in, but that didn't work. I couldn't get in the right position to get any leverage, so finally, in desperation, I put my fist through the window and cut my wrist very badly in the process, nearly severing an artery. But I finally managed to squirm out through the broken window and then pulled the unconscious Felix out and away from the car, which I expected to blow up at any second. But I found that the dripping was not caused by gasoline but by water dripping from the still-spinning wheels. By this time I was a bloody mess from the cut on my wrist.

Just at that time—which actually was only a couple of minutes after we went off the road—a new 1938 Oldsmobile pulled up. There were four white people in the car, two men and two women, and one of them grabbed my wrist and said, "Let me look at that. I'm an intern, and so is my friend here, and these two girls are nurses."

I said, "Okay, mister, but how about looking after my friend?" The other intern and one of the nurses went over to Felix, and I saw he was starting to move and breathed a sigh of relief.

The intern whistled when he saw the depth of my cut. "Good thing we came along," he said. "An artery bleeding like that is fatal in fourteen minutes!"

In a few minutes the intern had stopped the bleeding with a tourniquet and I noticed that Felix was standing. The intern who had been looking after him said he was okay. He was just shaken up and had a knot on his head.

"Okay," the intern who had helped me ordered. "Both of you get into our car. We'll drop you off at a hospital to make sure you're all right."

But I was a bloody mess and didn't want to dirty up their car. "I can't get in your car like this," I protested. "I'll just mess it all up. Besides, we don't have any money for hospitals."

"Look," the intern replied, "don't worry about messing up the car. We can clean it up. You might die if you don't get attention. You know, I just saved your life, but I won't get any credit if you go and lose it on me."

His warm and friendly grin convinced me, so I said, "Okay, Doc, you're the boss."

And the whole thing was so unnecessary. In the first place, the man who ran us off the road showed an utter disregard for our lives, our property and our rights. And this is what is the matter with so many people. And in the second place, it was foolish of me to panic and put my fist through that window. But that's what fear can do to a person, and I learned a valuable lesson from this experience, because the panic caused by my fear almost cost me my life. Actually, I could have opened the door with the inside handle, because it wasn't jammed, after all. And because the car was upside-down, I had just been turning it the wrong way. That's what fear and panic can do to you.

And so our benefactors dropped us off at a hospital in town, and although the interns and nurses had treated us very nicely, I still had doubts as to how we would be treated at the hospital. But again to my surprise, the white doctor was very kind and friendly and sympathetic. He was a boxing fan, but I was not well-enough known then for him to know about me, but he was a great Joe Louis fan, and I knew enough about Louis and the fight game to talk in a knowledgeable way to him.

"How about me, Doctor," I asked him. "Will this cut hurt my boxing?"

The good doctor shook his head. "Not at all," he replied, "if you take care of it. Keep it clean and change the bandages every day so you won't get an infection, and just don't use that hand much until it's well." He looked at me over his glasses. "Of course, I don't have to remind you not to hit anybody or anything including glass windows with that hand, at least not for a while, do I?" He smiled at me.

I smiled back, feeling all warm inside at the kindness shown me by the doctor and the two interns and two nurses. These people didn't care that I was a black man. They were medical people—healers—and the color of a man's skin wasn't the important thing to them. The important thing to them was to heal their patient. If more people thought like that, this would be such a nice world to live in. I don't know whether God is white or black, but this event proved to me that He truly made us all.

I was deeply impressed by this event. I felt that God had sent these people to save me—that it was no coincidence that four people trained in medicine came by just when I needed them. And I was impressed by the fact that these people were white and had stopped to help two blacks who were complete strangers. It dramatically proved to me that there were good people and bad people among all races—and that the color of their skin or their religion was not the point to judge them by. It was their actions that counted.

The car was not badly damaged and Felix soon repaired it, so we pushed on. Our small bankroll was rapidly evaporating, and when we arrived in New Mexico we were broke and hungry, so Felix called his wife, who was working in La Jolla, California, and she sent us $10, but by the time we reached Flagstaff, Arizona, we were again out of money, so Felix pawned most of his tools to get gas money and a little food. We managed to reach San Bernardino, California, and again ran out of gas, food and money. Felix then sold his last possession, a spray gun, and obtained enough money for another tank of gas, which was enough to get us to La Jolla.

Felix had been given the name of a promoter in San Diego by the name of Linn Platner, so we drove the few miles to San Diego to see if Platner could get me some fights, but we found that to our dismay, the Coliseum, where fights were held in San Diego, had burned down just the day before.

We were able to locate Mr. Platner, however, and he turned out to be a pleasant and friendly man, an influential and civic-minded citizen. He took the burning-down of the Coliseum calmly, considering that it held great importance in the city, being much in demand for boxing as well as for other events. I found that Platner's interest in boxing was for the sport aspect and the human interest he had in fighters. Money was secondary to him, and this in itself is unusual in the fight business.

We had met Platner in a bar across from where the Coliseum had been just the day before but was now a smoldering ruin, and he suggested that we go outside to talk and get away from ears that had no business hearing *our* business. So we stepped out on the street to talk, and Platner put a hand on my shoulder and looked me right in the eye and asked a direct question. "Can you fight?" he asked me.

For a second I was a little taken back by the directness of his question, but then I realized he wasn't trying to be funny or smart or a wise guy but was just trying to find out real fast if I was a man or just a smart-aleck kid.

"Yes, sir, I think I can," I answered very respectfully. Platner smiled and said, "I want a man who can fight and doesn't have to be pampered and babied. You've had sixteen fights, and you've done real well in them, but for the most part they've been prelims or club fights. Can you handle a main?"

"Yes, sir," I replied. "I'm certain I can."

"I like your confidence," Platner said. "You know, somehow you make your confidence believable without being cocky or boastful about it. And you're polite and courteous. I like that too. I get kind of tired of these fighters who feel that they have to act like pugs or tough guys."

"Thank you, Mr. Platner," I said. "That's the way I was brought up. People show me respect, and I give it right back to them. And, Mr. Platner," I went on, wanting to strike while the iron was hot, "I'll put up a real good fight for you. You won't be sorry. Really."

Platner patted my shoulder. "I believe you," he said. "I'm going to continue my operations in Lane Field, a 10,000-seat ballpark, and I'll find a good spot for you. Okay?"

"Fine," I replied, and Felix and I went home happy in the thought that we had a friend in the boxing jungle who was going to help us.

And help us he did. Platner's first promotion featured former light-heavyweight champion Maxie Rosenbloom against Odell Pollee from Philadelphia, and this was held on May 20, 1938. I was matched in the semifinal against Jimmy Brent and knocked him out in less than two minutes of the first round. I was all for fighting Rosenbloom next, but the former champion had other commitments, so Platner matched me with Ray Vargas, whom I knocked out in three rounds. The sportswriters were beginning to sit up and take notice of me by this time and gave me good write-ups. I was finally on my way. I was then matched to fight a lefthander by the name of Johnny "The Bandit" Romero, who had fought most of the better fighters and had a reputation of being a hard puncher, but he was erratic, turning in great performances sometimes, and mediocre ones at others.

For the first three rounds I had full control of the fight. Even though Romero was a southpaw he presented no problems, because he was too busy defending himself against the barrage of punches I was throwing. In the fourth round I decided to set him up for the finish, but I forgot for just an instant that Romero was left-handed and caught a solid left to the jaw and went down, hurt and dazed. Felix shouted at me to stay down for a nine count, and to make sure he raced around the ring apron and, reaching through the ropes, grasped my trunks and held me down until the count had reached nine, at which time he let go and I got up, still dazed. I saw Romero coming at me and through a fog saw that pulverizing left hand coming at me again, and although I ducked, the punch caught me on the temple and I went down. This time I got up at the count of eight and the bell rang, saving me from further punishment. That was all I remembered until the beginning of the eighth round, when I suddenly came around while Felix was holding spirits of ammonia under my nose. I asked Felix if the fight was over and he told me that it was the end of the seventh round and that although I had won the first three rounds, Romero had won the next four. With three rounds remaining I felt I still had a chance to win the fight, so at the beginning of the eighth round I jumped off the stool, meeting Romero in his own corner, and I put my head on Romero's chest and pummeled him to the body with both hands. I continued to be aggressive through the remaining rounds, which I felt I won. However, the referee, who was the sole judge, gave the fight to Romero. My fans were not satisfied with this decision and a near riot broke out. I was quite disappointed. I felt that I could have knocked Romero out and was angry with myself that I hadn't. I also felt that I had let my race and my fans down, and I stayed in the dressing room for quite a while after the fight, not wanting to face anyone. After over an hour a reporter came in and told me that hundreds of my fans were outside waiting to see me, so I went out and was comforted by the cheers I received. I noticed that my fans were not just blacks. There were also many Mexicans and whites present, all of whom were shouting that the decision had been a bad one.

The newspapers agitated for a return match, particularly George Herrick, then a sportswriter for the *Tribune*, and finally the rematch was set for that fall, when the rebuilding of the Coliseum would be completed. I had received $276 for the Brent, Vargas and Romero fights, which covered a period of about a month. The money was split with Felix, which left me with $34.50 a week to show for my efforts. So while I had achieved a degree of fame and popularity, I had very little to show for it financially.

While waiting for the Romero rematch, I fought Johnny Sykes and knocked him out in one round. Then I fought Lorenzo Pedro, a former holder of the state light-heavyweight championship, and won a unanimous decision over him.

Finally, the day of the Romero rematch came and we shared the same dressing room. He tried to butter me up by telling me that he had a warm feeling for black people. But I told him that I would try to knock my own brother out if I met him in the ring and that I felt I was going to knock him out.

There were about 3,000 fans at the fight. Romero landed the first punch. It was a vicious, hard shot to the stomach, and I was hurt, but Romero didn't realize how badly and failed to follow up his advantage. I stayed out of his way and kept moving for most of the rest of the round, but toward the end of the round I suddenly moved in and knocked Romero down with a short, hard right-hand punch. For the next four rounds I had things going my own way, landing at will on Romero. In the sixth round I knocked Romero down again, and in the eighth he threw a vicious left at me, but this time I was ready and stepped inside the punch and knocked him out with a sharp, hard right-hand shot.

This sensational victory gave me national recognition. I then went back to St. Louis, as I wanted to visit Auntie and bask in the warming glow of success among my old friends in my home town. It gave me a lot of pleasure to visit Auntie and be able to give her some money, and the pride I saw in her eyes also made me feel good. I was pretty pleased with myself, but I think any youngster would have felt the same way. After all, it was a long way from the "school." I looked up George Porter, partly because he was a good friend and partly because I wanted to rub it in a bit about what he said about the West Coast fighters slaughtering me.

"Hey," he said when we met, "you did real good out there, didn't you?"

I tried to be modest about the whole thing, but I don't think it came off. "Not too bad," I said.

"Come on," he said, "don't give me the humble bit. Five knockouts in seven fights ain't bad. And that Romero is no pushover."

"You better believe it," I said. "He hits like a mule. He

clipped me twice with that left of his, and I didn't even remember anything for the next four rounds."

George's eyes widened. "No kidding?"

"No kidding. That guy can hit. And in our second fight he drilled a shot to my belly that almost came out my back. If he had known how bad I was hurt then, he could have come in and finished me off. You know, George, in this game you've got to be a finisher. You've got to polish a guy off when you've got him in trouble, but you've got to be methodical and make each punch count and hammer him down—beat him right into the canvas."

That second Romero fight had really put me in the limelight. In November and December of 1938 I fought Ray Lyle and Irish Bob Turner in St. Louis, winning both fights by knockouts in the second round. These wins strengthened my reputation and popularity, and the St. Louis newspapers were lavish in their praise of a hometown boy. Things were looking good. I was sailing along in high gear. I felt that a championship, fame and fortune were just around the corner. Little did I realize the problems ahead of me—a very near brush with death, frustrations, hunger, disappointments and the slippery glass mountain I still had to climb before realizing my ambitions. It's just as well that people can't foresee the future.

FIFTEEN

●

Through the publicity I had received, I met Mr. Edley
Shipman. Mr. Shipman was an insurance man and lived
in St. Louis with his wife, daughter and son-in-law, Paul
Duke. Duke was a husky, good-looking young man who
liked to fight and had ambitions to become the heavyweight champion of the world. He had done well in the
amateurs, but he needed teaching and seasoning to get
anywhere in the pros, so Shipman came up with an idea
and approached me with it.

"How would you like to let me manage you?" he
asked.

"I've already got a manager," I told him, "and he's also
a good friend of mine."

"Felix Thurman?"

"Yes," I replied defensively. "I know he doesn't know
a lot about fight-managing, but he's learning, and he's
honest, and he has my interest at heart."

"Well, this is fine," Shipman said, "but I can assure you
that you'll get an honest deal from me, and besides, Thurman isn't here and I am, and I can get you a lot of good
fights in the East. And not only that, but I would like you
to train Paul and teach him things that would help him to

become the heavyweight champion, and I'll pay you extra for that."

"How much?" I asked, weakening. Shipman had been nice to me and given me small amounts of money at times.

"Five hundred for starters," he said.

That was big money to me then, so I told him, "Well, you'll have to work it out with Felix."

"No problem," Shipman told me. "If Felix doesn't agree to go along with the proposition, the whole thing is off. I'm sure he wouldn't stand in the way of your getting ahead."

Knowing Felix for the great guy he is, I knew he wouldn't stand in my way either, but I felt that I owed him a letter explaining the situation, and he agreed.

Joe Louis was the champion at the time, and while I agreed to train Paul Duke, I knew that he would never have a chance to beat Joe, because the Brown Bomber was in a class by himself. But I thought, well, I would do the best I could for Paul. He was a nice young man and it was a good arrangement.

George Porter went with us, and we drove my Oldsmobile to New York. On the way a truck rammed us from the back but luckily nobody was hurt. It wasn't bad enough to keep us from driving the rest of the way to New York, and we had a lot of fun on that trip.

When we arrived in New York, Mr. Shipman had a bit of a problem finding a place to live that would accommodate our black-white mixture, but he finally located a place for all of us in a nice apartment that overlooked Central Park. We rented two rooms: one for Paul Duke and Shipman, and the other for George Porter and me. The food was excellent, and we lived very near to the Pioneer Gym, where I worked out and taught Paul. I worked out with an old-time boxer named Billy Jones, a real good boxer who had fought in Australia and was a light-heavyweight. I was still only a middleweight but had developed a really savage punch, and I sure gave the poor guy a lot of trouble in our workouts. Another fighter I worked out with was Heywood Storey, who claimed to have knocked Joe Louis down in a workout. That, of course, means nothing even if it is true, which it could be—because there isn't a fighter who ever lived that couldn't be knocked down if caught right. It's how a fighter reacts *after* he has been tagged that separates the men from the boys. The guy who can come back, you know, after he has been jolted a good one, is a long way toward becoming a champion, and I'll go so far as to say that a fighter who lacks this ability to come back won't get far in the fight game. I also worked out with Eddie Mader, who had fought Joe Louis and Tony Galento. But I made a mistake in my gym workouts that a manager with more experience than Shipman had would have warned me about. I was looking too good and punching too hard in my workouts, and I became a fighter that managers avoided signing their boys against like the plague. They knew that I could take their bread and butter away from them in a hurry, as I became known as a spoiler. This didn't bother other fighters too much, but it did scare their trainers and managers, and in a way I couldn't blame them, because in one fight I could ruin a fighter's career, and the manager and trainer had a lot of time and money invested in their boy and didn't want to see it all go down the drain overnight.

Shipman tried to get Bill Duffy to handle me in the hopes that he could get me some fights. Duffy had been the manager of former heavyweight champion Primo

Carnera, the huge Italian whom Max Baer made mince-
meat of and took his title away. But Duffy and Shipman
couldn't get together on terms, although Duffy seemed to
want to handle me.

I did fight an exhibition with Paul Duke at the New
York World's Fair, and George Porter fought on the same
card, but I didn't get too much action the rest of the
time. But then suddenly my luck changed. I heard that a
man named Jack Richardson was interested in taking me
to Australia for a couple of fights, so I lost no time in getting in touch with him. I drove back to St. Louis and
found that Richardson had sent me a train ticket for San
Diego, so before I knew it I was back in that beautiful
city. Richardson bought my contract from Felix Thurman
for $250, and we were all set to shove off for Australia.

Meanwhile, I met a girl in San Diego by the name of
Mattie Chapman and we fell head-over-heels in love. We
decided to get married and then spend our honeymoon in
Australia. She seemed to be just what I was looking for in
a woman, and we hit it off real well and were all excited
about spending our honeymoon in Australia. But it just
wasn't to be, as Jack Richardson wouldn't allow it, and
leaving Mattie at the docks in San Pedro just three days
after our marriage was a heart-tearing thing.

You see, Richardson, who was an automobile salesman,
had coveting eyes for a good fighter, and he had heard
things about me which made him want to get me under
contract. Jack, I suppose, was what you might call a
fighter who had taken quite a bit of punishment in his
day as a young fighter. I suppose he was more or less a
glorified preliminary fighter. His greatest claim to fame
was that of having sparred several times with Pal Moore,
who was a fighter of note around Memphis. Anyway, Jack
bought my contract from Felix Thurman, and in securing

the contract for the Australian tour he inserted the clause that there was transportation for four persons, and I was to get $2,500 for two fights. This was a nice sum of money in that day for two fights, plus the fact that I would get transportation, and I felt that two of the four passages would be for me and two for Richardson. But he said that only one was for me. And still using the systematic way of moving a fighter around, Richardson brought his son and his wife with him while my wife was standing on the docks and my heart was breaking on the ship. I had gotten married to Mattie on January 4 in 1940 and sailed on January 7. I didn't even get a chance to know my wife. She was young and I was young, and we had agreed that she would let nothing prevent me from getting to the championship of the world. However it was bad business. It was my first bad-business venture, because I should have demanded that my wife be allowed to go. I never quite forgave Richardson for that.

It was a racist Australia I went to. Of course, visiting Americans of a celebrity stature, people like the Mills Brothers, Bob Parish—a great tenor singer—and others, were accorded privileges, and this gave a false image, because when the people asked how things were in America the usual answer was that everything was fine. They would say the black man—the Negro, as we called him at that time—was not in such bad shape. But even in that day, 1940, there was unrest among the blacks. And all the state-department heads, you understand, and the ambassadors overseas, they tried to quiet this thing down and tried to smooth this image over with visiting celebrities— black celebrities who toured abroad, musicians and dancers and actors. This was a way of keeping the other black people in a state of mind in which they would think that blacks were being treated royally. But they didn't know that these were the highly successful blacks that were traveling, and that there were thousands and thousands and thousands of blacks that were unsuccessful and were getting their lumps economically and socially, but as soon as a black got in the newspapers, people began to extol the great principles of the United States without realizing how fortunate he was to be able to have the unusual ability to break through that barrier that prevented so many blacks from seeking professions, and not only seeking professions but making contributions to succeed in professions that they sometimes were aware of but that somehow or other they always found that block—that roadblock. For example, like in Mississippi, Arkansas, Lester Maddox country, etc. Well, these were the things that were faced by the black man—these were a *few* of the things. Nowadays it is more or less subtle, de facto, and a person has to be on the alert at all times. The gentleman's-agreement thing is going on and is hard to overcome.

I was inexperienced and just out of St. Louis myself, a recent escapee from Mississippi, and I didn't know how to handle these problems. But I had a lot of things to distract me from these things on my voyage to Australia, which lasted twenty-one days on a Matson liner.

I was impressed when we got to Honolulu, where we made our first stop for fueling and taking on more cargo and discharging some passengers. En route, we were traveling with a troupe of stage people—I think it was the Orpheum circuit—and I made friends with a lot of people, which was not hard to do, because show people are very easy people to travel with. We were traveling cabin-class and had our little fun in cabin-class, because the people who were from the first-class were kind of stiff-necked. They often came down to watch our entertainment. This was where they came to hobnob and rub shoulders with celebrities. Then at night they would go back upstairs and eat in their own dining room.

While leaving Honolulu I was impressed by the boys diving off the deck of the ship and into the blue waters for coins. We had stayed over all day and all night, and we left when the sun was setting. It was quite impressive and the people on shore were putting leis around the necks of the passengers and saying *aloha*, which means "come back again." And as the ship pulled out, Hawaii began to diminish in the background in the sunset, and as the horizon grew higher and higher, Hawaii seemed to sink and sink, and pretty soon we saw the sun just peeping over the ocean. It was kind of sad as we heard the Royal Hawaiian band in the background playing "Aloha Hawaii," and we were in the shadow of night, and there were vast waters stretching all around us.

I think a man never gets so lonesome as he does on the sea as he watches all that vastness. He realizes how near to nothing one human being can be. And as the strains of the music finally died down, I could hear the steady, reassuring and rhythmic rumble of the ship's engines. It was an experience that I'm glad I didn't miss. I would even have fought for nothing just for that experience. The only thing that made it so very sad for me was the fact that my lovely bride of three days was not there to share all these beautiful things with me. I've always said, although I doubt whether I'm the first or only person to say it, that pleasures are for sharing, and a pleasure or happiness not shared is really no pleasure or happiness at all.

We finally arrived in Samoa and were met by Polynesians. We were getting farther and farther away from civilization, for Honolulu was like a Midwestern city. We now saw girls walking around in *lava-lavas*, with their breasts uncovered. It was beautiful, and nobody seemed to pay any attention to it, because this was the usual way that the people went around.

We were treated royally. The ship docked out a-piece, and we came in on motor launches and toured the island a bit, but it rained every five minutes. It sprinkled and dried. Sprinkled and dried. Sprinkled and dried. It just didn't do for a man to wear a good suit of clothes. He would be far better off if he just wore a bathing suit all the time.

So we spent the day there and sailed at nightfall, this time without the aloha band playing and singing, but it was still beautiful the way the natives waved good-bye to us. They stood and waved, and everything was in the sunset, as we were going south. And again my thoughts went back to Mattie, and I thought how wonderful this all would have been to share with her.

A few days later we came into Suva, Fiji, and there I met a Negroid type of person—the Melanesians. These people, in that day and time, 1940, had the same hairstyle that is so popular with the blacks today. The bushy hair that's combed straight up. Some of them had hair that was almost a foot high on their heads. It was crinkly but beautifully done and neatly trimmed. I couldn't understand how they could comb their hair that way and have it look so beautiful. I had no notion to comb my hair that way. I was following the white man's trim at that time, processing my hair by using a type of thing that would straighten it out. You see, I was brainwashed too—Western style. This is the way that show biz was, and this is what the black in America had begun to do years prior to that time, because you could not find a musician who would not use the so-called gas on his hair. They called it different names. Processed something or other you might call it. It was only a method of straightening hair with caustic. And in my mind it was that caustic that has been the cause of many black fighters suffering severe eye damage. Because that caustic in the hair, regardless of how good you think you washed it out, there was perhaps some left in the scalp, and when an athlete really got to sweating, trickling of the remnants would drip into the corners of his eyes and damage their structure. I've seen more blind black fighters than blind white fighters, so I've surmised this. I know too that it will cause one to go bald quicker.

These Melanesians were English-speaking people and they invited me to one of their feasts—just me and none of the others. Being a black man, they were quite interested in seeing me, and even more so when they found that I was a boxer. These people were pretty ardent Joe Louis fans, and the fact that they had another black American fighter right there in their midst made the feast quite a gala occasion, and they treated me like I was visiting royalty, which I have to admit made me feel pretty good. The other passengers were taken on the usual tourist tours complete with guide, but they didn't get to see the things that I did. When they invited me to their village I thought that, well, here goes some of my hard-earned bread and that they would really sock it to me financial-wise, but I was wrong. They didn't charge me a penny. They just wanted me to be their guest—just to honor me, as they figured that I must really be a good fighter to be sent all the way from America to Australia to fight.

In 1960 I heard from a man who had met me to take me to the village. He had read an article about me and still remembered me after all that time. I couldn't hardly forget him either, you know, because this man had no arms. His arms were bitten off at the shoulder by a shark. They're great shark-fighters, these Melanesian people are—both boys and men. They would hunt sharks with only a knife, and a shark had happened to catch this young man and bite both his arms off. However, as people do out of desperation when it's a case of life or death, he called upon great hidden strength and managed to somehow get to shore. A person, out of desperation, can fight and do more things than he can imagine, and this is why I say that any boy can—any*body* can—because if they have guts, and people do have guts, they can do many, many things they thought were impossible. How this man got out of the water after the shark bit his arms off, I don't know, but he did, I guess by calling on this inner strength born of desperation and his will to live. And here he was—living to tell me about it. Now, this was tremendous, and he didn't feel sorry for himself. He had no artificial arms to feed himself and for the most part fed himself by holding his head down to his food, more or less like an animal, you see, but he was happy. I mean he seemed to be satisfied with his lot, and he took me up to this village and showed me how they bake pig and potatoes underneath leaves. And they had an unusual way of getting a drink. A boy would run up a tree—and I mean he actually ran up the tree. The tree was bent at an angle, and he ran up the tree with his hands and feet—and these people had big feet—and they had hard calluses on the side of their feet; these were so well-developed that they were more like muscles, and this helped them to climb. The boy would take a knife out of his belt and cut a cocoanut off and come back down. Then he would take the knife and cut the top of the cocoanut off with one clean swipe and hand it to me to drink the fresh juice.

The food was delicious, and I ate like there was no to-morrow. And most of their food being starchy, I was con-tributing to a weight problem I would have trouble with later. After the feast they danced for me and played man-dolins and other stringed instruments—I think they were tiples—and strangely enough, their music, although prim-itive, bore a strong resemblance to Dixieland jazz and had that spiritual rhythm of the Negroes. I felt happy and at ease with these people, and it became a page in my book of memories that I shall never forget.

We never stayed in these places overnight. We always sailed just before the sun went down, and so a few days later we found ourselves in New Zealand, and here there were the Maori people, and like all these countries, they were white-dominated. I didn't have fun there like I had on Suva. When the passengers on the *Monterey* found out how the natives had wined and dined and feted me on Suva because they regarded me as a great fighter, their own respect for me shot up and I became quite popular among my fellow passengers, who now regarded me as a celebrity. And to be honest, I liked the feeling of being important and recognized by my fellow men as one who had made his mark in his profession. And I don't think this is egotism. I think it is quite natural, and anybody who says they don't like the thrill of recognition—well, there has to be something wrong with him, because it just isn't natural for people not to like adulation.

Well, anyway, here we were at Auckland, New Zea-land, and we did a little souvenir-hunting there, and the surprising thing to me was the great number of nationali-ties there and their ability to adapt themselves to the for-eign way of life and the language and to prosper. It was raining quite a bit in Auckland, and I didn't particularly like it there.

This was not too far from Sydney, Australia, so we came into Sydney Harbour a few days later. We saw the city, and it was sitting kind of like on the side of a hill, and we saw the city long before we got to it. We saw the red tile. I never saw so many red-tile roofs. You might have thought you were in South America or Mexico. Those red-tile roofs were beautiful, and we finally came into customs and everybody ate their breakfasts quickly because there was this usual excitement to get ashore when we arrived at a new port.

To our disappointment there was nobody there to meet us; certainly not the welcome I had expected. And then I realized that I was just another American fighter arriving in Australia; that I was just part of the cargo arriving— and this deflated my ego a bit, you know.

Finally, Harry Miller, a secretary from the boxing promoter's office, arrived to meet us, but he really came to meet Jack Richardson. I was just a property, and this is what is so sad about being in the boxing business. Richardson secured an apartment for himself and his family in a place called Bondi Beach, and I was living in King's Cross, which is what you might call downtown, miles away from where Richardson was living. The gymnasium was not too far off from where I lived, and my hotel was in the center of town, where the shopping district was, and the harlots, the hustlers, the seamen and all the transient people were a conglomerate there—actually it was what you'd call the sin-city area, you know.

One day as I was walking along I saw two black men across the street, and they were dressed like fashion plates out of *Vogue*. I introduced myself to them, and when they told me they were Johnny Hutchison and Al Brown, I knew who they were. Johnny was a great little fellow out of Philadelphia, a featherweight who had fought many of the better fighters in the featherweight and lightweight divisions, and he had been in Australia for about a year. The other fellow, Al Brown, was a bantamweight, and they were stablemates and sparring partners although a division apart in weight. Both were fine fighters and very popular. Al could do any kind of a dance there was at that time. They invited me to their apartment to talk with them and play records, and I had two or three records of my own that I had brought with me. One was called "Jumpin' Jive," by Cab Calloway. We had a nice little feast, because Al was an excellent cook. He cooked some down-home foods, and I felt quite at home.

We met another fighter over there, a Hawaiian fighter. He didn't want to be classed as a black. His name was Danny La Verne, and he was later killed in the war. Danny was of mixed parentage—one was black and the other Filipino. He was alert and a good fighter, but he looked askance at Johnny and Al, as though they carried some type of contagious disease. He just didn't want any part of being black. I guess he was ashamed of his heritage. This is one of the main methods that the white man has used throughout the years to divide the blacks. To tell one group that they're better than the other because of the texture of their hair, the color of their skin, you know. They infer that you're not really black because you're not like them, and so egotistical are the men and women they're talking to that they begin to believe this and alienate themselves from the blacks. This has been a system down through the years, and so the white man could easily divide and conquer the blacks by keeping them fighting one another.

I'm happy that now a bond has come about among the blacks. That they finally have come to identify with one another by, for one thing, wearing their hair bushy, and I was against this wearing of the bush at first until I began to see what it was actually doing—making black people feel proud of what was theirs. This hair is theirs, and they'll have it as long as they live. They can curl it and fry it and dye it or do anything they want to, but as long as they live it's theirs, and I believe that what God gave a man he shouldn't try to change.

I wasn't trying to impress Johnny and Al. They had never heard of me. I was just trying to get out there and make good because I was out to make a buck—like the contract said—$2,500 for two fights, and I was out there trying to make a reputation so I could come back and really win the championship of the world. Because I knew that I was ready to fight for the championship even at that time. Remember, I had been boxing ever since 1935, you see, as an amateur, and as a professional since 1936, and here it was 1940, so I had put in over three years as a pro. I thought I was ready for a championship match.

The first thing I was ordered to do was to settle in my quarters at the hotel, but I didn't like the meals, so I got an apartment right across the street, and that left me living one block down the street from where Al and Johnny lived. They had two apartments there, but they lived in the same building, and being on the same block, we could get together and have bull sessions.

Of course, Danny La Verne lived in another part of town. He didn't want to be associated with blacks, you know. So Johnny and I would go to the gym together to work out. Johnny was a tremendous fighter. I used to love to watch him work because he had such great class and style, and I guess I had things that Johnny liked. I was a tremendous puncher with both hands, and I tried to pat-

tern my fighting after two or three fighters. I tried to bob
and weave like Jack Dempsey, and I tried to hit like Joe
Louis, who was coming along in a grand rush at that time.
Louis was, in fact, the champion then, and we were near
the same age, so I wanted to be the only middleweight
who could perhaps outhit a heavyweight, and being the
puncher that I was, I had no trouble getting opponents
on the floor, and this made it hard for me to get men to
work out with.

After a few days in Sydney, Richardson came along
and took me to see a fight between Ron Richards, who
held the middleweight, light-heavyweight and heavyweight titles of Australia, and an Australian contender by
the name of Fred Henneberry. Richards, a short time before, had beaten Gus Lesnevich very badly, and Lesnevich was later to become the light-heavyweight champion
of the world. Richards had a tremendous punch that
could blast a guy clean out of the ring and was a dangerous and much-feared fighter.

The Australians were great people for gambling, and
the betting was quite heavy on the Richards-Henneberry
go, so a strange thing happened. You see, they have a rule
that in the event a fight is won on a foul, all bets are off.
So they fought for ten tough rounds, and Henneberry,
seeing that he couldn't go much further, as he was taking
a severe mauling, fouled Richards in the eleventh several
times, and so the fight was awarded to Richards, but all
bets were off because of the ruling. Of course, this made
some of the fans very angry, but those who had bet on
Henneberry were quite happy.

Jack Richardson asked me if I thought I could take Ron
Richards and I told him that I thought I could if I was in
real good condition. The easy and bountiful living aboard
ship had put on extra pounds that I was having trouble

shedding, but I finally convinced him, so he said that I would have to go out into the country to train and whip myself into shape.

And so, Richardson also hired a trainer for me—a Jewish man by the name of Ike Kutner, and this was one terrific guy. His only interest was getting his fighter in the best shape possible and having a winner. Money meant nothing to him, whereas producing a winner meant everything. He had a small pension coming in because he was a war veteran, and he just wanted enough money to pay his rent and food, with enough left over to get a beer once in a while. A beautiful man, and he helped me get in shape.

We went to a place in the Megalong Valley and set up our training camp there. It was just like a ranch. Not a fighter's ranch, but just a regular ranch, and people used to go to places like this on holidays and eat scones and drink tea and have a restful time away from the city, even though it was just for a short time. This training in the country was a new and delightful experience for me, as I had always done my training in sweaty gyms. Actually that smell didn't bother me—in a way it became a rather pleasant smell, because this is what boxing was made of: sweat and hard work.

At the ranch I got to know the family I stayed with real well. One of the boys was named Bill, and he was young like myself, and the other boy was named Red, and they were sheep- and cow-herders. They had some horses, and I used to go riding and escape from the training monotony. These people were just so nice to me, and I had Ike Kutner there. I was quite happy and contented.

When I used to do my roadwork I would go from the Megalong Valley—which was in what the Aussies referred to as the bush, which was located in a long valley

—and I would alternately jog and walk up a steadily winding road of seven miles every day to the closest town, which was Black Heath. This was on top of a 7,000-foot mountain, and that fresh, sweet morning air was so delightful that it really defies description. I was enjoying my roadwork. And pretty soon I'd find myself up on top of this mountain, and I'd walk in this store and get a plate of ice cream in the morning before breakfast. I'd get seven scoops of ice cream in chocolate, vanilla, strawberry and whatever else they had, and I'd take my time and eat them with a cookie or two, and then I'd walk on back home, so that would make me do fourteen miles a day. It was truly beautiful. I wasn't used to this luxury kind of training, and when I'd get back to the ranch it was like twelve o'clock. Sometimes I'd hitch a ride partways back. It was not a much-traveled road, so I didn't get many rides, but this was good, because I got myself in tremendous shape. And this solitude gave me time to think and dream and make plans for the future, and I was feeling at peace, finally accepting the fact that Mattie wasn't with me. There just wasn't anything I could do about it right then, so there was no use of me ru-ining my health fretting about a situation that I had no power to change. You know, there is a wise saying, a prayer I guess you'd call it, and it goes something like this: "God grant me the strength to change the things I can that need changing; to accept the things I cannot change; and the wisdom to know the difference!"

Richardson was in town, so I was out in the Megalong Valley by myself with Ike and these young people, but during the day they were out doing their chores, so they were not with me and I trained furiously. Sometimes I'd go out and chop wood. And I had a lot of time to think about my little bride. I used to try to imagine what she was doing. And I'd imagine how I'd make some money and send it to her, and how she'd save some money, and how we'd open some kind of a small business together. And then we'd have some children while we were still young, and then the children would grow up with us, and this would be fine. This would be lovely. This was the way that I had planned it. However, this was not the way it was to be.

SIXTEEN

•

It was while training in the Megalong Valley that I met the aborigines, a remarkable people who are, as the name implies, the original people in Australia. They inhabited Australia and lived there in harmony with nature.

These were interesting people, and through them I received some help in solving my weight problem. You see, I learned that the aborigines made fast trips through the bush going long distances, and yet they carried no water and only a few strips of meat. They were all quite lean and possessed tremendous stamina, and they attributed all this to the fact that they would chew on these strips of meat, chewing until the last bit of juice had been extracted. This would nourish them and keep up their strength without adding any weight. They never swallowed the bulk of the meat from which they had extracted the juice. So I figured they had something and decided to try it, and I found that in about a week I had lost a couple of pounds and still felt strong. That encouraged me to keep at it. Later, when a reporter asked me how I had made the weight and I told him about it, he didn't believe me. But that often happens when one tells the truth, and I didn't mind, as long as I was getting the job done.

You see, my weight problem was different than that which most people are faced with. Every pound on my body was solid and hard, and getting rid of any of this was the problem. It wasn't fat or liquid, which is what most people get rid of when they start dieting or exercising to lose weight. My weight-losing experiences in the past had been disastrous. One time I had been told that taking Epsom salts would do the trick, so I tried it, and lo and behold it worked. The only problem was that after the first round of the fight I had lost weight for, I was so weak that I could hardly get off my stool to answer the bell for the second round. This fight was against Billy Sims, and in the first round the only thing that had saved him was the bell. But in the second he almost killed me due to my weakened condition, and in the third they gave Sims the decision because I was too weak to raise my gloves to hit or to defend myself. So you see why I was a little bit cautious about heeding the aborigines' advice. But after losing the first couple of pounds and still feeling fine, I kept on with it. And I implemented this with a diet plan of my own, a plan that I used successfully for the rest of my fighting career, especially when I fought as a heavyweight and maybe a month or two later had to come down from 185 or more to 175 in order to defend my light-heavyweight title. With this plan I was able to do it easily and without losing my strength, so in part I have the aborigines to thank, and in part I have to shed the mantle of modesty and give myself the credit.

Of course, this chewing meat without swallowing it is not an easy thing to do. It takes great control to keep from swallowing a delicious piece of meat instead of just chewing on it and swallowing the juices before spitting out the bulk. And it is not a pretty thing to watch either, so I ate alone, but the Baptiste family, with whom I lived, understood. I continued on my plan, but at first it nearly drove me out of my mind. I would cheat a little and sometimes "accidentally" swallow a succulent piece of meat, but as I found this and my own supplemental diet working, I became encouraged and determined and the "accidents" became less and less frequent.

So you see, these "uncivilized" people had something their more "civilized" brothers didn't have. They knew, in their primitive way, how to get by on a fraction of the food that we did and live a healthier life. They had become well-adapted to their environment and had no food or financial problems, so I guess there is something to be said for their way of life. Their rugged overall good health and apparent happiness attests to this.

And so I was getting in good shape, you see, but before I could take Richards on I fell sick with a virus and the fight had to be postponed. After I recovered they decided to match me against Jack McNamee. Now, McNamee was a good fighter who had beaten my early boyhood hero, Alan Mathews. It was Mathews who had helped set my style, in fact. McNamee had beaten Mathews. He had shut Mathews' eyes up with stinging left jabs, and Mathews' manager thought he could use one of the tricks that the old-time fighters in the bare-knuckle days used, by cutting underneath the eye and letting the blood come out so that it would open up and relieve the swelling and the fighter could see. He took the scalpel and cut the muscle loose under Matthews' eye, and his eye hung. It was an accident, of course, because the manager felt that if his fighter could see he could have beaten McNamee, who was a six-foot-two-inch youngster who could jab like fury. Mathews was game enough and could take him out if he could hit him, but he couldn't see him.

So I had to box McNamee, and knowing that he had

stopped Alan Mathews gave me all the incentive in the world to place a kayo on him. I barrel-housed McNamee and hit him around his body until—as he later stated in the papers—it felt like I was pouring hot lead in his stomach. I stopped McNamee in four rounds.

So the fight was all set with Richards in Rushcutter's Bay, an indoor arena, and we drew a capacity crowd of 15,000—due to my disposing of McNamee in such handy fashion and Richards' great popularity. This Rushcutter's Bay stadium was in downtown Sydney, and it was where Jack Johnson had fought Tommy Burns and won the heavyweight championship after chasing him all over the world. He finally cornered him in Sydney and won the championship there and became the first black man ever to win the heavyweight championship of the world.

Ron Richards was a fighter who was very much feared in that day. He had beaten Lesnevich, who went on to win the light-heavyweight title a few years later. Lesnevich, you understand, was one of the main people that refused to fight me, to give me a chance at the championship. We had fought common opponents, and the Ron Richards of that day beat Lesnevich into a jelly. He busted him up like a crate of eggs and put Lesnevich in the hospital.

And so the day of the Richards fight finally came. The newspapers had played up a feud between Richards and me, and this is all right, I guess. It filled the stadium. In fact, Richards turned out to be one of the cleanest-fighting and most gentlemanly men I have ever fought. Finally, all the formalities and introductions were over with, the referee gave us our instructions in the center of the ring and we touched gloves and went back to our corners. I shuffled about and threw a few warm-up punches at an imaginary opponent as I waited in my corner. At last the bell rung and the adrenaline was really flowing as Ike Kutner patted me on the back for luck with the final admonition to watch out for Richards' tremendous punching power. Well, I was so eager that I guess I just paid no mind to Kutner's warning, and when we met in the middle of the ring I jabbed once, very casually, and Richards threw a right-hand blast that exploded against my jaw with the force of an atom bomb. I felt like I had been kicked in the head by a mule. I literally saw stars and red, white, purple and orange rockets were shooting off in my head as I hit the canvas. I could taste blood in my mouth and was furious with myself at my carelessness. Through the buzzing that was going on inside my head I heard a big groan come up from the fans, like they were thinking, "This guy is nothing. Just another hamburger from the States." And I could hear shouts of "Fake! Fake!" from the fans who were disappointed at the prospect of the fight ending so soon. Well, I'll tell you something. If any of those people had been on the receiving end of that punch they wouldn't have been yelling at all. You know, I can still feel that punch. I was hurt bad and had enough experience in the fight game to know it, and I knew that I had to get up and that my work was cut out for me if I was to make a decent showing. Just losing to Richards wouldn't have been so bad if I put up a good fight, but to get knocked out in the first round—in fact, in the first minute of the first round—that would have been bad for my career. Even though Ike Kutner had warned me about Richards' punching power, I just hadn't believed that a man could hit that hard. But I was in good condition. I had trained hard and faithfully, and this, plus my pride and the fact that my future was at stake (and the booing of the fans), goaded me to get to my feet. I went into my defensive shell, peeking out at Richards from behind protecting gloves and forearms. I back-ped-aled and clinched. I didn't throw any punches—I was just trying to stay alive, and that wasn't easy to do, as Richards was throwing barrage after barrage of shattering punches at me. I was catching most of these on my arms, shoulders and gloves, but occasionally one would slip through my tight defense and rock me some more. Rich-ards was throwing real hot leather at me, but I managed to survive his crushing punches and soon discovered that he was primarily a puncher but was not too strong in the boxing department. So I moved around a lot, forcing him to box, never giving him time to get set to throw his heav-iest punches, as he had to get set in order to launch these. So I began to shape up and he began missing me in my desperation defense, backing away, covering, clinching—just trying to keep from getting knocked out while my head cleared.

By the third round I had my jab working to the point where I got his nose bleeding, and by the fifth had opened up cuts over his eyes, thus slowing him down con-siderably. By the seventh I knew I had him, and from then on it was just routine. He was bleeding all over the place, and I was hoping that the ref would stop the fight, because I didn't want to see this courageous guy take any more punishment, but he wouldn't stop it. I had to go on hitting Richards, because as long as he was in the ring with me he was dangerous and could take me out with one punch. So I hit him like he was a sandbag, and I did everything but knock him down. I was banking shots off his head with right-hand leads, so finally Richards was so badly cut up that the fans started to cry, "Stop the fight! Stop the fight!" and Joe Wallis, the referee, stopped it. The way they stopped the fight there, the ref would step in and tap the winner on the head.

The next day the newspapers there showed a picture of me on the deck and the caption ARCHIE MOORE GETS OFF THE FLOOR TO STOP RICHARDS. This was a very proud moment for me, and I knew that I was on my way, beating the triple-crown-holder like that. After all, he held the middleweight, light-heavyweight and heavyweight championships of Australia, and this built up my prestige tremendously, although none of his titles were at stake in our fight. But now, overnight I had become a big name in Australia, and, as a matter of fact, I had made quite a ripple internationally and my services were in demand.

I was booked to fight Atilio Sabatino on May 9, 1940, in Sydney. I planted a few red-hot left hooks on the Puerto Rican's head and stopped him in five rounds. I then knocked out Joe Delaney in seven rounds. My next victim was Frank Lindsay, whom I kayoed in four rounds in Tasmania. Then, on June 27, 1940, I was booked to fight Fred Henneberry in Sydney. Henneberry was Ron Richards' toughest and most feared rival. He was a desperate, hard-fighting Australian who would do anything in his power to win a fight, and he was made a solid favorite over me in most of the dispatches, but when I fought him I hit him everywhere but on the bottom of his feet, knocking him out in seven rounds.

My rematch with Richards was held in Rushcutter's Bay on July 11, and I felt sure that I had his number. The only problem was that for one of the very few times in my life I let someone tape my hands, a ritual I usually performed myself. I had such complete faith in Ike Kutner that I entrusted him with the job, and in the rush and turmoil of getting to the crowded arena and dressing room, we had very little time and Ike taped my hands too tightly. I should have insisted on doing them over, but the fight was ready to start, so I thought, well, it would be all right this time and let it go. But it turned out that it wasn't all right, as I broke my left hand in the second round.

In this second fight with Richards I was the favorite. I had the respect of the fight fans after my six straight sensational wins in Australia, and my name was something to be held in awe. I found this second fight much easier even after breaking my hand. I had to fake my left jabs and just use my right hand for the most part, and I cut Richards the same way as I had in the first fight. I bewildered him, I bluffed him, mainly because I had scored such a sound beating over him in the first fight. I bluffed my way through and won the twelve-round decision fighting one-handed. Then, after revealing that my hand was broken in the fight, I decided it was time to leave for home, not particularly because I wanted to have more fights but to see my wife. I had not seen her in about six months. How would I find things when I got home? I began to worry. But all doubts were wiped away by the thoughts of the perfect harmony we could enjoy if she had done just some of the things that I wanted her to do.

SEVENTEEN

•

I had left a reputation in Australia that would stand for years to come, having won all seven of my fights there, and all against top competition. I was booked to come home on the *Monterey* late in 1940. I was glad to be coming home. Now I would see Mattie again. There were big training expenses that fighters are afflicted with, so when I left for home I had only $800 in cash to show for my efforts in Australia. But at least I had enhanced my reputation to the point where I was now nationally and internationally recognized. At this time, Hitler was at war with the Allies, and the United States ordered all its citizens to return home. Richardson had already left with his family for the safety of the States, although actually it wasn't until a year later that America became involved with the bombing of Pearl Harbor.

Due to the danger from submarines, the *Monterey*'s course was changed, and we went to Tahiti, a beautiful spot where the people were quite gay and happy and the girls wore sarongs and had flowers in their hair. Our arrival was greeted warmly and in festive fashion. The value of the French franc had dropped considerably, so I guess the sight of our American dollar had a bit to do with the enthusiasm of the natives. On board with me was a boxer by the name of Fighting Carlos, who had left because with the likes of Al Brown, Johnny Hutchison and Danny La Verne no longer being in Australia, the abilities of men like Fighting Carlos were no longer in demand. So Carlos was on the *Monterey* with me, and he was imbibing considerably. He had roughly $400 in his pocket when he left Australia, and he changed $100 into a thousand dimes and began to play the slot machines. So, intrigued by the winning sequence the machines provided for him temporarily, he changed the rest of his money into quarters and began to play the machines furiously. He played and won, and lost and won, then lost and lost, and his hand blistered and swelled up. On the way to Tahiti there was an opportunity for some of the fighters from foreign countries to fight the Tahitian boys, who were thought very well of by the natives. And Carlos, although quite pickled, decided to take on a fight and pick up a few quid. However, he picked up a real tiger, and not only did the boy punish Carlos, but he made him quit. I was Carlos' "manager," so I tried to collect his purse for him, but the promoter ran out with the money and he never got paid, so I advanced Carlos $50 so he could get on home, as he had lost all his money playing the slot machines on ship.

Before we left Tahiti I had a weird but memorable experience in Papeete, some parts good and some parts bad. A French sailor had given me his cap for a souvenir and I was walking down a sunny, gay street wearing it when a group of about twenty-five French sailors who had been drinking spotted me and challenged me as to where I got the cap. They intimated that I had stolen it, and one large and particularly belligerent sailor tried to snatch it off my head. I ducked under his grabbing hands, and as I did one of his buddies aimed a kick at my stomach. I partially blocked this with my left hand, which still was in a cast. Now, there's supposedly some rule against a professional fighter using his fists on somebody because they are classified as deadly weapons, but that's the only weapon I carry, and although I'm not going to look for trouble I figure I'm entitled to defend myself, ruling or no. So I spun around and uncorked a beauty of a right at the guy who had just kicked me in the stomach and he went flying about three feet backward and hit the deck like he had been pole-axed. The sailor who grabbed at my cap was swinging a left at me. I bobbed under that one and smacked him along the side of the face with my cast-heavy left arm and he went down.

By this time the rest of the gang of sailors was getting pretty perturbed and were using their *sabat*, or foot-kicking type of fighting, and their fists, and some of them had belts with heavy buckles that they were trying to dent my skull with. I was really keeping busy, swinging with my right because my broken left hand was aching pretty bad, and I knocked a few guys down, but I receipted for a few kicks, punches and belt-buckle nicks in the meanwhile. I thought my number was up for sure, as there seemed to be more sailors by the second. Fortunately, I received aid from an unexpected source just when I thought that all was lost. About a dozen big Tahitians rushed in to help me, and those guys were rough. They used their fists, judo and feet, and before long the mob of French sailors was in full retreat, dragging their wounded along with them. And, believe me, they had plenty of comrades to drag off the battlefield. I didn't want any more of that kind of action myself.

Well, as we got closer and closer to home I became happier and happier at the prospect of seeing my bride again after our long separation and short three-day hon-

eymoon. I was feeling in great spirits. I had a few dollars
in my pocket, had bought some expensive perfume and
other presents for Mattie and had established a nice reputation I hoped to capitalize on in the near future. Everything looked roses. But I was doomed to have a great disappointment. Mattie and Richardson were waiting to
meet me on the dock. But it soon became obvious that
Mattie wasn't as happy to see me as I was to see her. I
could sense that something was amiss by her lukewarm
greeting.

"What's the matter, honey?" I asked her.

"Oh, nothing," she replied, hardly looking at me.

"It's got to be something," I came back. "Come on,
baby, let's hear about it."

"I've been sick," she said finally. "I was in the hospital
and had an operation."

I was stunned. "Operation?" I managed. "Why didn't
you write and tell me about it?"

"Well," she said, "I didn't want to spoil all that fun
you were having over there."

"Fun? Heck, I was working. Trying to make a future
for us. Sure I had some fun too, but that was just something that happened along the way. You know we agreed
that nothing was to stand in the way of my getting to a
championship."

She didn't answer me.

"Well, didn't we agree?" I insisted.

She nodded her head.

"Let's get on home," I said finally, deeply hurt and disappointed by the whole scene. "You know," I told her,
"you should have told me if you were sick. I would have
dropped everything and come back to you. No money in
the world could have kept me away if I had known."

Well, that perked her up a little and she gave me a little smile.

"You know," I told her, "I didn't come back with a lot of money, but I do have a beautiful reputation and a nationally known name. I'll really be able to make some money now."

Mattie nodded and Richardson drove us back to San Diego from San Pedro, where the boat had docked, and took us over to Mattie's house. Then he left, going out to his home in Hillcrest. Now I was back in the inner city again, at Mattie's house this time, with her and her father and mother and brothers and sisters. I was greeted lukewarmly, and this was all right, you know, as far as I was concerned. As a stranger coming into somebody's house, I didn't expect to be greeted enthusiastically. I took Mattie downtown in a pickup truck and bought something like $35 worth of food to eat, because inasmuch as I was staying there I wanted to pull my own oar and not be sponging on them.

At that time, costs for room and board were about $125 a month, and when I bought $35 worth of food, it almost took up the whole truck to take that much home the way prices were in those days. Bread was two loaves for 11¢, eggs 19¢ a dozen, bacon 29¢ a pound, three cans of Pet milk were 11¢, oranges were a penny each, you know, and prices of this range, as everything was in abundance and cheap—so we got all these groceries and steaks and took them home. Then after a while, when we were sitting around, everybody began to slip off, and they'd be gone a few minutes, and before I knew it everyone had eaten and nobody had offered me anything to eat, and I was very put out about it, so that night I didn't stay there.

I was thoroughly confused, and Mattie and I never

really got together after that. Our break-up started from that moment. I asked Mattie for a divorce so I could be free to marry someone else, but it never really panned out until I married Joan Hardy in 1955. Joan is one of the most beautiful women I have ever seen, and I am grateful that my prayers were finally answered and she became my wife. She's a wonderful wife and mother, although at first people gave us two years together. But now we've got two daughters, Rena and Joanie, and three sons, Hardy, D'Angelo and little Anthony. And we have a great adopted son, Billy Daniels, so I'd say that the marriage was still together, and the only thing that can break us up is death.

Joan is my right hand when it comes to business and finance. She handles my phone calls, appointments, correspondence, contracts, income tax and any other matters that arise, such as acting as hostess, greeter, etc. She's quite a lady, and I love her and our children with all my heart. The night I met Joan was a lucky one for me, as I am now a very happily married family man.

My first bout after returning home from Australia was against Pancho Ramierez in San Diego, and I knocked him out in five rounds on October 18, 1940. My next fight was against a tough little scrapper by the name of Shorty Hogue in San Diego, and he decisioned me in a six-rounder on December 5, 1940. It was getting to be a habit with this guy, because he had outpointed me on December 21, 1939, before I left for Australia, but it really was no disgrace losing to him, as he was very good and one of my toughest opponents. In January of 1941 I knocked out Clay Rowan in San Francisco in one round, then came back to San Diego to tackle Shorty Hogue once again, and again he decisioned me, this time in a ten-rounder. Eventually, I was to get a measure of revenge on Shorty, but fate decreed that wouldn't happen until over a year later, and in the interim I was to have a very close brush with death, a brush that could have ended my boxing career even though I survived it.

My next bout was a rematch with Clay Rowan in San Diego, and I again disposed of him in one round. I then fought Eddie Booker, another of my all-time toughest opponents. I fought him on February 26, 1941, in what almost was the last fight of my career, but instead proved to be the first of a series of tough fights.

I came out of my corner for the Booker fight, took one casual look at Eddie and landed a right to his jaw. He fell face-forward with his feet up in the air, so I thought that this Booker was an easy touch and that if I hit him again the fight would be over real quick and the fans would think this was a turkey that Linn Platner had promoted and boo, so I thought maybe I'd ease up on him for a few rounds. But before I knew it, Ed was up and clawing at me and had me fighting for dear life. Before the fight was over I knocked him down two more times, but each time he got up swinging before he was halfway off the canvas. I hurt my hand again during this fight, and I was fortunate to get a draw with Booker, even after knocking him down three times. This man was a real tiger, a real gutsy fighter, because I tagged him real good several times, and he not only refused to stay down but came back at me like he was going to blast me clean out of the ring.

I fought Eddie again in December of 1942, and again we battled to a draw. Then, on January 21 of 1944, Eddie placed a kayo on me in Hollywood. So what can I say about Eddie Booker? He was one of the great fighters of my time. Many people have asked me who was the greatest fighter I ever fought, and for practical purposes I might say Rocky Marciano, because this was a sensational fight against a sensational champion, and it was a tough fight; or I might say my toughest fight was against Yvon Durelle, when I had to get off the seat of my trunks four times before I was able to knock him out. Granted, these were tough fights, and my first fight with Durelle has to rate as one of my toughest come-from-behind fights. But I think that in his time, Eddie Booker was every bit as great as Rocky Marciano was in his time. And there was another man, Charley Burley, who was a great fighter, but the younger crowd has never heard of these fighters. Another great fighter was Ron Richards, the hard-hitting Australian triple-crown-holder whom I beat twice. So Burley, Booker and Richards have to be three of the greatest fighters I ever fought, and we met each other when we were in our prime, whereas I was past my prime when I fought Marciano and many others.

Fighting Charley Burley was almost inhuman, because he kept punches coming at you like a riveting gun beats a tattoo on a rivet. He was a human machinegun, the way he kept those punches spouting out, and nearly as dangerous. Perhaps you wonder why Burley didn't get further in the ring. Well, there's a long and sad story behind that, but I'll make it brief. Charley Burley was selling the daily *Pittsburgh Post-Gazette* and the weekly *Pittsburgh Courier* around Pittsburgh. In his spare time he worked out with Jack Zivic at the Zivic gymnasium. Run by and for the Zivic family, this gym soon developed into a special place for Burley to pass the time. He listened and watched as older brother Pete Zivic and Luke Carney, a talkative Irishman, merchandized the title-contending Fritzie Zivic all over the continental United States—beating the canebrakes and whistle stops from Podunk to Kalamazoo and from Grand Rapids to Ogden. On occasion the operation landed in big cities like St. Louis or Chicago, and it was in the latter that Fritzie was knocked out by Laddie Tonelli on October 25, 1934, in three rounds, although Fritzie got his revenge on Tonelli by kayoing him twice in 1936.

Burley's success in the hotly contested gym workouts as he ran through the Zivic stable—which included another white hope in the embryonic stage named Billy Conn—was soon the talk of the black community. Al Abrams, then a youthful and erudite *Post-Gazette* sports editor, gave plenty of ink to the Hill boys, who could fight up a storm. Most of them were under the banner of Gus Greenlee, owner of the famed Pittsburgh Crawford's baseball team. In the Greenlee stable at that time were Pittsburgh Jackie Wilson (a featherweight champion to be), Honeyboy Jones, Red Bruce (a terror whom middleweights and light-heavyweights feared), the great light-heavyweight champion John Henry Lewis and others. Not only did Greenlee have talent, but he also had a big bankroll. Meanwhile, Fritzie accepted Burley's challenge—after Charlie had made numerous previous ones without getting anywhere.

Fritzie was beaten by the wiry and deadly twenty-year-old Burley in a June 13, 1938, showdown, and again on July 17, 1939, as Fritzie Zivic found himself on the receiving end of Charley's jabs and body slams—punctuated by rights to the head.

I remember how strange Burley looked—so youthful, so handsome—trying to look older by penciling a thin moustache between his lip and nose. His thin legs, however, reminded me of a stork. Burley knew he was a future boxing great, a champion. He marched over to Greenlee's Crawford Grill and asked for proper representation as a professional fighter, but Greenlee was not in a negotiating mood. After all, Greenlee had the mighty

John Henry Lewis and an assorted stable of fistic preda-
tors, plus the swanky Crawford Grill, so he was not interested in adding Burley to his fight stable. Burley really
wanted Greenlee to handle him, but underneath, the
spindly fighter had pride—and still has pride today—so
he did not pursue the matter further with Greenlee.
Youthful pride sometimes operates as a deterrent. In this
case it may have cost boxing a star of the first magnitude.

Instead, Burley signed with Luke Carney, the manager
of Fritzie Zivic. Eventually, on October 4, 1940, Fritzie
won the world welterweight title from Henry Armstrong.
However, under boxing's restriction that does not allow
two men under the same management to fight each other,
Burley's hopes were shattered by the contract with Carney. Burley beat many great fighters, including a huge
220-pound Texas heavyweight, J. D. Turner, Jack Chase,
Leon Zorita, Holman Williams, Harvey Massey, Bobby
Millsap and Cocoa Kid, but never could get a shot at the
championship. Through the best years of his life, he
watched Fritzie Zivic, the gladiator whom he had
soundly beaten, earn many, many thousands of dollars,
along with the plaudits of the fans.

Tommy O'Loughlin, a fight manager out of Minneapo-
lis, secured the contract of Elmer "Violent" Ray. Ray had
beaten Jersey Joe Walcott and had scored victories over
other fighters of stature. Watching his career wash out
toward the open sea like a ship without a rudder, Burley
took Ray on in a gym workout. Burley's left snapped
Ray's head back. Ray threw a left hook, but Burley
leaned his serpentine body back, giving himself position
for the counters that were to follow. Burley stepped in,
knuckles down, and shot his right hand straight into Ray's
meaty jaw, following with a whistling left hook. The hook
was on target, and with jaw-breaking force. Ray's wide

shoulders were the first part of his body to hit the floor, his large feet coming down as an aftermath, and the resin dust rose slowly as a hardly distinguishable snarl—or it might have been a smile—creased Burley's countenance as he once again proved his punching power over a much larger opponent. But this was small satisfaction to Burley, as his career ended soon after without his ever getting a chance at the coveted championship.

If Fritzie Zivic can be applauded as a celebrity in Pittsburgh, and if Billy Conn can command a $12,000-per-year job in Pittsburgh recreation, is it not reasonable that a great fighter like Charley Burley be granted his due after a lifetime of murky twilight?

The Charley Burley story is further proof of the creed of the Any Boy Can clubs that "any boy can succeed if he wants to and receives help in time." Charley Burley wanted to succeed, but unfortunately, he did not get the help he needed.

EIGHTEEN

•

The day after my February 1, 1941, fight with Eddie Booker, I was in my front yard, raking leaves in the pleasantly warm sunshine, waiting for my girl friend, Catherine Turner, to show up for our date. Catherine and I had been seeing each other steadily, but inasmuch as my first marriage had wound up so badly I was in no hurry to get married again, and Catherine, being the understanding woman she was, never tried to push me into anything. In the back of my mind I thought that eventually I might marry her, but I wasn't rushing it.

As I worked in the sun, the world seemed quite rosy to me. But all of a sudden I felt like a red-hot iron had been thrust into my stomach. I doubled up in pain as sharp, unbearable spears thrust through my middle, then I fell to the ground, writhing in agony. At first I thought that perhaps Booker had injured me somehow in that area and that this was a delayed effect of his blows, and I twisted with pain as I broke out into a sweat. I was sure that I was dying. My auntie saw me out there lying on the grass and immediately called an ambulance and sped me to the hospital.

I remember the agonizing ride to the hospital and the even more agonizing examination by the doctor, and what seemed to me like stupid questions that I couldn't answer. But now I realize that they were not stupid questions and that these people were trying to help me. At the time, though, everything seemed stupid to me, as I was in such excruciating pain. After the examination and tests, I remember the doctor saying that I had a perforated ulcer and that I would have to be operated on immediately if I hoped to live. Even in my pain and foggy state of mind, I thought of what this could do to my career, so I pleaded with the doctor to make the incision in a certain way that I had heard about from another boxer who had undergone abdominal surgery. It had been successful with him, so the doctor agreed to do it that way.

The next thing I knew I was given a spinal anesthetic and was numb from the neck down. I was determined to live through this and resume my fighting career as soon as possible. I've always had faith in God, and I've always had faith in myself. When I was on that operating table I glanced over at the little bellows that registered my breathing. It began to quiver, and I felt that I was dying. I prayed and asked God to give me a chance, because I knew that I was not too young to die. Many people had died much younger, but I wanted Him to give me a chance to help my auntie, who was getting along in years. She had been wonderful to us and had devoted her life to raising us. And there was my little niece, June Williams, who was only nine years old. I was their only means of support, and I prayed to God to let me live so that I could help them. And God was with me, because the last thing I remember saying was, "I've got to live. I've got to live. I've got to live." And five days later I woke up. I had tubes in my nose and was being fed intravenously through my feet and arms.

Big Al Hinson, who is now a high-ranking officer in the

U.S. Army, came by to see me. At that time, Al was an orderly in the hospital. He wanted to be a doctor but didn't have the money or the funding to go to school, so he was an orderly. He asked me how I felt. I didn't even recognize my own voice when I answered him, it was so low and weak, but I told him that I was all right. He told me that he had dropped by several times in the past few days and that he thought they were going to have to take me out in a basket. He told me that he had never seen anyone with as much fighting spirit as I had.

After being flat on my back for several days, I began to wish with all my heart that I could sit out in the sunlight and watch the sun. If I could sit on the porch and breathe some pure air that didn't have the antiseptic smell of a hospital, if I could see with my own eyes the sun coming up early in the morning—this would be beautiful. So beautiful. How I wished for the natural things that people take for granted: to be able to walk around, bask in the sunlight, breathe fresh air—to get a drink of cool spring water. These things I wanted more than anything. The best things in life are free.

And all the time I was lying there I never gave up the idea of a boxing career. This was my life, and I was determined to get well and become a champion.

After I had been in the hospital for a while I learned that I had been in a coma for five days, hovering between life and death. Peritonitis, which was very often fatal in those days before the discovery of some of the "miracle" drugs, had set in and been further complicated by pneumonia. I finally overcame these complications and began a long recovery period. I tried to relieve the monotony of hospital routine by forcing myself to relax thoroughly, and then through my thoughts to escape from the situation I was in, and I found that these two things not only

helped me during my recovery but also throughout life.
And so it came about that I found two new and meaningful words for myself—"relaxism" and "escapism," which
I give a great deal of credit to in helping me throughout
my boxing career as well as other aspects of my life. You
see, while flat on my back in that hospital I had nothing
much to do but think. Up to now, most of my thinking
had to do with boxing, but now I found myself taking in-
ventory of myself. I felt that I had direction and a pri-
mary purpose in that I was aiming for a boxing championship and a good family life and financial success so I
could do things for my wife and children and the underprivileged. I had to recover my health so that I could accomplish these other goals. I was puzzled as to how a
clean-living athlete like myself could come down with a
serious case of ulcers, because I had always been of the
belief that ulcers came from drinking and improper living. But to my surprise I found that the greatest cause of
ulcers was tension, worry and frustrations that cause
more amounts of acid to be released into the stomach
than is healthy for it. An overabundance of acid can literally eat a hole in your stomach lining. So now I had to dig
into my own character and find out what was causing me
to do these things in order to stop them and prevent a re-
currence. My "escapism" and "relaxism" helped, but I
still had to get at the root causes of my tension and worry,
and I found to my surprise, after a self-analysis, that
down deep inside I held bitterness in my heart. This was
what had caused that excess flow of deadly acid in my
stomach and brought on my problem. You see, bitterness
is not only a character-wrecking emotion, but a health-
wrecker as well, and the only thing a person can accomplish by harboring this terrible emotion is to wreck his
health and character. I had been bitter and frustrated be-

cause I had always had such a problem getting anywhere in the fight game in spite of my ability, and this had rankled me and made me bitter. I had been destroying myself without even knowing it. This is what happens to many people, and this is what happens to a lot of blacks —who through the years have had good cause to be bitter. But they must realize, as must all people, that bitterness and hatred are destructive forces, you understand. And they are especially bad for an athlete who wants to be a champion and needs everything going for him.

I also took stock of my assets while I was in the hospital. My main one was that I was still alive, and next was the fact that I was a skilled fighter with many Godgiven talents and that I would be able to fight again, although my doctor advised me against this, and my auntie agreed with him. So I worked hard and got rid of my bitterness, and this has stood me in good stead throughout my boxing career as well as throughout my life. My mastering of "relaxism" and "escapism" were two other good things that came out of my ordeal in the hospital. Through practice, I can take a five- to fifteen-minute nap even in Grand Central Station that will leave me as completely refreshed as a good night's sleep would for many other people.

Diversion, of course, is a must if one is to relax and escape. I don't care what it is; it could be golf, tennis, swimming, collecting stamps, photography or whatever. I found my route to "relaxism" and "escapism" through music, and I recommend this most highly to anyone. Whatever you find most interesting and pleasing is okay, but do it and you'll see your mental attitude change for the better. You'll become a happier individual, a more successful individual, an easier-to-get-along-with individual.

Other things that helped put my mind at ease were that Dr. Pollack, who had operated on me, assured me that I would be okay, and that Linn Platner, the fight promoter, was beautiful to me. Not only did he visit with me and cheer me up and reassure me, but he sent a specialist to check me over and the specialist confirmed Dr. Pollack's prognosis.

I felt that besides changing my attitude through "relaxism" and "escapism," my physical fitness due to rigorous training for boxing had helped me. But I felt that the biggest factor in pulling me through was my faith in God. Without His help I would never have made it.

There was a beautiful tree right outside my window, and as the sun rose in the morning I would watch as its rays reflected off of the dew-laden green leaves. I longed so much to sit in the sunshine and breathe that cool, fresh morning air. After a while I became tired of the drab, bland hospital food and talked my auntie into bringing me some ice cream, which she did every day when she visited with me. Then she began bringing me chicken broth. After a while I convinced her that I needed some of her delicious fried chicken, and she brought me that. Of course, the doctors and nurses didn't approve of these things, but I attribute the regaining of my strength to these measures.

I was in the hospital for thirty-eight days, weighing 163 pounds when I went in and a mere 108 when I left. I was completely out of funds when I left and still had a long period of recovery ahead of me before I could become productive. My dear friend, Catherine Turner, helped me both financially and mentally, knowing that worry was the worst thing in the world for an ulcer patient. I continued to practice my relaxing and escaping theories, doing this largely through music, my own imagination and my talks with Catherine. And I gradually built my weight up to 135 pounds, but could seem to go no further, although I ate well and rested most of the time. One day I was out for a drive with Catherine when I suddenly had another severe pain in my stomach. I was gripped by despair, you know, because I thought, well, here we go again, and I didn't know how I could make it through another ordeal like that. Catherine drove me to the hospital right away, where the doctor diagnosed my illness as acute appendicitis. I was operated on immediately, but this time the illness was not nearly as severe, and in a few days I was back home. I then began to gain back my weight and in a short time was up to 155 pounds.

I now felt it imperative that I get a job so that I could support my auntie and myself and repay Catherine. I was referred to a man by the name of Milton Kraft, a champion fly-caster who was a great sports enthusiast and a big fan of mine. He gave me an easy job as a night watchman, as he knew that I was in no condition for heavy work at that time. I gradually grew stronger and started doing light exercises and walking, and then I started trotting. At this point I felt strong enough for heavier work, so Milt gave me a job mowing grass. This paid more money, and the exercises helped me to build up my body and legs.

I eventually worked myself into fighting condition, and with the help of Felix Thurman's ingenious "license-plate protector" to help protect me against blows in the area of the scarred tender section of my body, I was ready to resume the battle after almost a year of enforced idleness from the ring. I have already given the details on the special protection Felix worked out for me, so I won't go into that again, except to say that in my first bout since becoming ill I knocked out Bobby Britt in three rounds in Phoenix, Arizona. I followed this by knocking Guero

Martinez out in three rounds in San Diego in February, and then knocking Jimmy Casino out in five rounds in San Francisco.

Mattie and I had decided to again try to make a go of our marriage, and Catherine, whom I felt I was eventually going to marry, graciously stepped aside, as she wanted to give Mattie a chance. But it just wasn't to be, as we argued continually. I don't think it was her fault or mine. There was just a personality clash here that couldn't be bridged, although I still think that if there hadn't been that long separation after only three days of marriage, things would have been different between us. There just was no communication, and we were like strangers. She seemed disinterested in my stories about my adventures in Australia and about my boxing, and we seemed to be unable to find a common ground between us. So once again we separated, this time for keeps. Mattie has since passed away. She was a fine person, and I always felt that she deserved a better lot.

NINETEEN

•

Fights were getting scarce in San Diego, and what with my break-up with Mattie and all, I felt that a change of scenery was in order, so when Felix suggested that we go to Oakland I was all for it.

We had very little money between us, so we had to plan to do things in a very economical way until I could get some fights. I put $35 down and bought an old panel truck, and we fitted out the rear with mattresses and an old ice box, and this became our home for the next few months. We planned to get a monthly parking deal at a lot near the gym. In that way we would save carfare to and from training, and we would have free bathroom facilities.

When we arrived in Oakland, however, we stopped at a gas station on Franklin Street, and the owner of the station, Mike Segal, a former boxer, knew about me. When he heard about our plans he suggested that we park on his lot and use his bathroom facilities for a token fee of $1 a month, and we took him up on his kind offer. Our plan was for me to try and get fights, and if I didn't get a fight before too long, we would both go to work in the shipyard until I could get going.

We lived very frugally, as we had very little money,

and allowed ourselves 75¢ a day each for eating. I trained
very hard but was unable to get a fight. Our money was
running out, so Felix got a job at the shipyard. Felix left
me my 75¢ for food when he went to work, but one day I
got up and the usual stipend was not there. I couldn't
figure out what had happened, although I later learned
that although Felix was working at the shipyard he hadn't
drawn his first paycheck, as they always held back a
week's salary. But in the meantime I was hungry, and
getting hungrier by the minute. All I could think about
was food, and I envisioned all that beautiful food I had
consumed aboard the *Monterey,* and about Auntie's great
home cooking, especially her fried chicken, and I got
hungrier and hungrier. When Mike Segal came to open
up the station I could have bummed the price of a meal
from him, but I was too proud.

I heard that the railroad was hiring men, so I went to
the railroad yard at the foot of Fifth Street and saw about
fifty men waiting there. I fell in with them. Every now
and then a man would come out of the employment office
and say, "I need four number twos," or "I want three
chefs." Well, I waited around until finally the man came
out and said he needed a fourth cook, and when nobody
answered his call I figured that this would be my chance,
so I got up and followed the man inside. He didn't ask me
any questions about experience and the like, but just told
me what track my train was waiting on. I found that this
train was traveling between Oakland and Ogden, Utah,
and I felt that at least I could get a couple of meals out of
this before they found out that I wasn't a fourth cook and
fired me.

I boarded the train and followed some of the other
men who had been hired to the dining car. The man in
charge assigned them to their tasks. Then he asked where

"Forty" was (the nickname for the fourth cook). I didn't know that, so finally the man asked me what I was hired for and when I told him "fourth cook" he knew I was a greenhorn, but he was a nice guy and explained to me that a fourth cook or "Forty" was a pearl-diver—a dish-washer. Well, I wasn't too proud to take on honest work, and I was pretty hungry by that time, so I took it. After all, this wasn't the first time I had washed dishes. But I never realized that there were that many dishes in the world. We were on a troop train, and it seemed like all those soldiers did was eat. I could see dishes in my sleep, and the odor of food was in my clothes and my skin and my hair, and I couldn't even take advantage of all the good food and eat because the smell made me sick. After a few days, however, I got used to it, you know, and then I began to get my appetite back and enjoy the good train food.

I stayed on this job for several runs, and when I finally quit I had a full stomach and $100 in cash.

I went back to the gas station, where I had left the truck, but it was gone. Mike Segal told me where I could find Felix. At the same time he handed me a telegram from Linn Platner, the San Diego promoter, offering me a fight with Shorty Hogue in San Diego. I located Felix and learned that he had brought his wife and daughter to Oakland and that all three were working at the shipyard, making a combined total weekly wage of around $300, so Felix wanted to stay where he was, which I felt was a wise decision on his part. The fight game was exciting, you understand, but it had its ups and downs, and a man was better off in most cases to keep his stomach full by getting steady work in some other field. But this was not for me.

And so I returned to San Diego alone and fought

Shorty Hogue on October 30, 1942, gaining revenge for
my previous two losses against him by knocking him out
in the second round. A week later I fought Tabby Romero in San Diego and knocked him out in two. I was on
my way once again.

Realizing the insecurity of the fight game, I decided
that I wanted something else going for me, so I went into
the chicken-frying business. This was something I knew
about, as I had learned how to make delicious chicken in
the South. I borrowed $400 from a friend to get started,
as I couldn't get credit due to the shallowness of my security and the risk of being a boxer. I also felt that my color
had something to do with it. So I had to rely on friends
and went in on the shoestring capital of $400. I located
some chairs, tables, linens and silver in the want ads for
around $350. I borrowed a cash register and a weekend
supply of towels, soap, etc., and spent $35 for chickens,
cooking ingredients, a few steaks and turkeys. Now I was
in business. I managed to get hold of three waitresses and
a top-flight college grad for my maître d'. This young man
had personality plus and would have been tremendous in
anything having to do with public relations. He agreed to
work for me on a percentage and came to work in a tux
and cummerbund and was beautiful as a greeter. I envied
him, as I was in my chef cap and white-checkered uni-
form in the kitchen. It was quite a contrast, but I was
pleased indeed at the results of the first day, which netted
a grand total of $16.70, but the enthusiasm over the
chicken satisfied my ego, so I planned my strategy for
next week's accelerated business.

I opened at 11 A.M. and worked until 11 P.M. that Sunday and netted $51. Being a stout believer in advertising,
I took $50 of my profits and paid for an ad in the *San*

Diego Tribune, announcing to one and all that Archie Moore's Chicken Shack was open and one ould buy the World's Greatest Fried Chicken there.

The immodesty of the ad must have tickled the taste buds of the readers, for the next week they came in droves and the old borrowed cash register rang to the tune of $400 plus for the week. With this I paid back salaries and doubled the rest back into merchandise and hired a Jazz trio led by Peter Rabbit, a jazz pianist. Our take the first night he played was $370. From then on, word spread like wildfire and the advertising paid off, and this success laid the groundwork for many of my public explosions when I returned to boxing.

Not a day after that did we take in less than $700, and I had begun to make plans for expansion, but I remembered that I had not completed the four-line poem given me by my auntie. I had not yet done a good job in boxing. So I was tempted to go back to it and give up this $700-a-day business. I now had two goals, and I was having trouble choosing between being the world's champion chicken-frier and the world's champion boxer. Pardon my immodesty, but I am no doubt the chicken-frying champ, having developed the most scientific, nongreasy but juicy, tender chicken ever to sizzle in a cast-iron skillet. There has been an army of men who wanted me to go into the chicken fry business with them, and among them is my good friend Bruce Gelker, president of the beautiful Saddleback Inns of The Americas, who has been trying to get me to stop my youth work long enough to set up and market this great product nationally, with franchises, etc. No doubt Mr. Gelker, a former star athlete and already a winner in the world of business, can see what a great success this business could be. Perhaps I might involve myself in this venture with him. With my product and his great business know-how, I feel that success would be assured.

On the other hand, my mind—and again I hope you will pardon the immodesty—seems to be a regular idea factory. One of the things I have developed is an unusual and most revolutionary self-defense punching bag that is practical, and yet not without the Archie Moore humor, for I am a man who likes a good laugh and have even learned to enjoy a good laugh on myself. I think it is very important that a person be able to laugh at himself rather than at others. At any rate, my bag invention has Eastern people in the know in boxing, as well as leading toy manufacturers, sitting up and taking notice. For all the many years that boxing has been on the scene, no one has ever thought of this idea. But, then, the unusual is my bag, although there are times when some people find my ideas a bit humorous. However, as I mentioned, I learned long ago how to laugh at myself, and this is of great importance. But I have my serious moments, and I am very serious about helping youth and helping the United States save itself from itself.

Anyway, even though the Chicken Shack was prospering, I felt that I had to go back into boxing. I guess it was a challenge as well as anything else that sent me back to the rigorous grind of the prizefighter. Even after my kayo victories over such tough opposition as Shorty Hogue and Tabby Romero, sportswriters and fans were still a bit skeptical about my stamina after returning to the ring in less than a year after I had undergone extensive and severe surgery. They felt that I had not really been tested as to my durability since coming back, and most felt that a solid, hard punch to the area of my surgery would cripple me. So to settle the matter, Linn Platner arranged for me to take on tough and rugged Jack Chase, who had won his last 22 fights. None of the papers gave me a chance to win. In their minds it was just a question of how long I would last. My recent five straight kayo wins meant nothing to them, so I felt that the only way I could prove my point to them was by going the route with a top-rated fighter.

I caught Chase with a really solid left hook in the second round and put him on the deck. I felt that he was hurt bad enough right then for me to have gone and finished him off, but I purposely held back because I wanted to show everybody that I was ready to go all the way. I hurt his eye pretty badly, but I avoided hitting him there. I wanted him to go all the way with me, and he did, and I won seven of the ten rounds. Now I had proved to everyone's satisfaction that I was durable against tough opposition.

Richardson was still officially my manager, as he held my contract, but inasmuch as Felix Thurman was a loyal and good friend and had made my early comeback possible by his "license-plate protector," I felt that he should get another chance to manage me, especially now that things were definitely looking up. So I brought the matter up before the State Boxing Commission and they ruled in my favor, setting a price of $450 on my contract. So Felix once again took over my managership. However, although we still remained good friends, his ideas on my future did not exactly agree with mine, so he agreed to let me buy my contract back for the same price he had paid for it, but the price might as well have been a million dollars as $450, as I didn't have either. The problem was solved by Linn Platner. Since he was a promoter he could not buy my contract, but he had his brother buy it, and this was a good arrangement for both of us. I was a big attraction for Mr. Platner to have on his fight cards, and the fact that his brother owned my contract was assurance that I would get my share of fights. Things were beginning to look up, as all of us were now eating regular, and I was slowly repaying my debts to Catherine Turner and others.

On December 11, 1942, I had a rematch with Eddie Booker, and he was just as tough as ever. But I managed to get a ten-round draw with him. Then I was rematched against Jack Chase for the California middleweight championship at Lane Field, the ballpark used by the San Diego Padres baseball team when they were still in the minor leagues. The fight drew well and my share of the gate was over $700, quite a big payday for me. This was a tougher fight for me than the first go with him, and we fought in the afternoon, and here is where some of my studies about fighting and fighters paid off. I recalled a trick used by some old-timers when they fought outside in the daytime where they would keep their opponent facing the sun by some adroit maneuvering. I tried this with Chase, you know, and it worked. By the end of the fifteenth round, Chase's eyes were practically closed, so I didn't have too much trouble taking the decision and the title from him.

Later that same year I kayoed Eddie Cerda in three, then the following month put Big Boy Hogue to sleep in Lane Field in five. On August 2, 1943, I was matched for the third time against Jack Chase, this time in San Francisco. Chase was a good fighter, and by this time he was able to figure out my style. Without the sun to assist me, I lost a fifteen-round decision to him. I avenged this defeat by decisioning Chase in San Diego on November 26 of the same year in a torrid ten-rounder. I was to fight Chase twice again, several years later: In 1946 we fought to a draw in Oakland, but in 1947 I took him apart in Los Angeles, placing a nine-round kayo on him.

But going back to right after the loss to Chase in San Francisco, I had been after Mr. Platner for a really big-time fight where I could make some big-time money. Mr. Platner tried to get me a match with highly rated Ken Overlin, but he was unable to come to terms with Overlin's manager. The latest Chase fight in San Francisco had earned me nearly $500, but this was still peanuts in comparison to what many of the other name fighters were getting, and after paying the usual training expenses, supporting Auntie and repaying Catherine Turner, I had little money left. I was discouraged and puzzled by my inability to get in the big money like Sugar Ray Robinson and others, who were getting purses close to the $100,000 mark. And here I was, piddling around for $500 or $700, and against tough competition like Shorty Hogue, Jack Chase and Eddie Booker. The people Sugar Ray and the others were fighting couldn't possibly have been any tougher.

I was in a bad frame of mind, and after losing to Chase I dropped a ten-round decision to Aaron Wade in San Francisco. But I bounced back with a five-round kayo over Kid Hermosillo in San Diego on November 5, 1943. Then, after decisioning Jack Chase in ten on November 26, I knocked Amado Rodriguez out in one round in San Diego to start the new year off right on January 7, 1944. But 1944 turned out to be not one of my better years, as on January 21 the dreaded Eddie Booker knocked me out in eight rounds. Then, after kayoing Roman Starr in Hollywood on March 21 in two rounds, I faced the talented and terrific Charley Burley and he decisioned me in ten of the toughest rounds I have ever fought on April 21 in Hollywood. I followed this loss by decisioning

Kenny La Salle in ten and kayoing Battling Monroe in six, both fights taking place in sunny San Diego.

I then decided to go to New York, where I figured that I could get in on some of that big money that was floating around. On the way I stopped at Indianapolis, Indiana, to see if Hiawatha Grey would come along with me to New York as my trainer, but at the time he was training George Costner, so he declined my offer. Costner later fought Sugar Ray Robinson in a bout that drew a $90,000 gate, and Sugar Ray placed a kayo on him in one round. And so I pushed on, New York-bound, but on the way my car threw a rod and wrecked my engine to the tune of over $400. Not having enough money to pay for this, I left my car in Bedford, Pennsylvania, and took a bus the rest of the way to New York.

Jimmy Johnston was a colorful character who didn't smoke or drink, and when I walked into his office he was wearing a derby hat that was tilted forward on his head. I liked Jimmy Johnston right away. He told me he would get some fights for me and told me to go to the gym the following morning and really train in earnest, as he had some hot fights in mind. When I told him that I was broke he gave me $25 and told me that he would pay for my training expenses at Stillman's gym and give me $25 each week for expenses until I got to earning some money. At Stillman's, I met many fighters who were either famous or destined to become famous. I became good friends with Sandy Saddler, who was just starting out. And there was the great Jake La Motta, who was training there at the time.

Inasmuch as Jimmy Johnston was a matchmaker he couldn't be my manager, but he arranged for his brother Charley to manage me. I beat Nate Bolden in ten in New York on December 18, 1944. Then on January 11, 1945, I

kayoed Joey Jones in Boston in one. Then later that same
month I kayoed Bob Jacobs in New York in nine. In my
next fight I was scheduled to fight in the semi in Boston
against a fellow named Nap Mitchell out of Philadelphia.
When I entered the ring I was a bit surprised and cowed
by his size, as he was six-foot-four and weighed over 200
pounds, but I gradually cut him down to size and
knocked him out in the sixth. This was my third knockout
in four fights since coming East, and I was moving along
pretty good, but pretty soon I found that I was up against
that same old bugaboo: I had made the same mistake that
I had made on my prior visit to the East. I was looking
too good against bigger men, and managers began avoid-
ing matching me against their boys.

I was rematched against Nate Bolden on April 2, 1945,
this time in Baltimore, which was Bolden's home town,
and again I took a ten-round decision over him. Later
that same month I again fought in Baltimore, this time
against Teddy Randolph, who was a hard-punching,
crowd-pleasing scrapper. We had one whale of a fight,
and I put him away in the ninth. I continued to do well
for the rest of 1945 and wound up the year with a 12–2
record, and many of these fights were against top-ranking
men. But still I was unable to get a championship match,
although I was now gaining recognition as a leading contender for the title. In 1946 I had eight fights, winning 5,
losing 1 and drawing 2. My only loss that year was to Ezzard Charles—and I felt that I had beat him. However, I
was now recognized as the number-one contender for the
light-heavyweight crown, and I continued to be recognized as the number-one challenger for five years,
through the reigns of Freddie Mills, Gus Lesnevich and
Joey Maxim. But a title match was not forthcoming. It
seemed that everybody except Archie Moore was getting

a crack at it. I was mystified as to why I couldn't get a crack at the championship, you see, and I must admit that in spite of practicing my "relaxism" and "escapism" theories, I was becoming quite frustrated. Since Charley Johnston was unable to get me a championship fight I took matters somewhat into my own hands by putting on a letter-writing campaign to sportswriters all over the country. While they were on my side, they seemed powerless to help me.

In 1947 I won 7 out of my 8 bouts, and in 1948 I won 9 out of 13 fights. I was so disgusted that I was getting a little careless with my training, like in my first fight with Len Morrow in Oakland on June 1, 1948. Some false stories went out after that fight that I had accidentally fouled Morrow and that then when I had spread my hands to apologize he took advantage of my unprotected jaw and landed a haymaker. This is not the truth. I just wasn't in condition and had taken Len Morrow too lightly. I don't care how good a fighter is, he must be in top condition. Len Morrow beat me fair and square in that first fight. He was plenty good, and it took a good fighter in good condition to beat him.

Because Morrow had knocked me out, his manager, Alan Moore—who was an excellent manager for the Oakland boy—thought it best now to keep his highly rated charge away from me. And he did a very good job for about two years until Morrow got into an altercation with the Boxing Commission and they barred him from boxing in all NBA states. There were some non-NBA cities that were regarded as dumping grounds for fighters, and as was the custom, managers would bring their fighters into a town that had just enough fans to keep the doors of the arena open. Not enough to really make any money, but just to keep the doors open and keep the local promoters

THE ARCHIE MOORE STORY

in business and keep the big-name fighters coming to the town to fight nonentities who would pad their records for the time when they would fight in big-time matches in Chicago and Los Angeles and New York. This padded record would build these fighters up and help their drawing power.

And so Morrow had this trouble with this body of government appointees, and he found that these men knew very little about the physical aspect of the sport, as these were businessmen. In all honesty, I think that a boxing commission should be made up of ex-fighters as well as astute businessmen. In this way the boxer would have representation by people who know the game from the participation standpoint as well as men who are knowledgeable in the ways of business. Then a boxing commission would not only be able to protect the public against any shenanigans by boxers or their managers but can have regulations for the benefit of all. One of the things I feel should have been done ages ago is to insure each boxer against serious injury in the ring so that he and his family can have some security. But to get back to Len Morrow. After his falling out with the commission he had to fight in the non-NBA towns, you see, and there were only a few, like Baltimore, Los Angeles, Toledo and some small towns where you couldn't draw a telephone booth full of people if there was to be an execution. But Toledo was a town in which I had some of my most sensational fights, so I agreed to the rematch with Morrow in Toledo. I put in hard and determined training and destroyed him in the sold-out arena. In the tenth round, a round that almost proved fatal to Morrow, for the first time in my life I seriously hurt a man. A clean puncher, you understand, a snappy puncher like me, rarely is a killer in the ring. He rarely injures anyone seriously, because the speed with which he delivers his punch causes a shock that takes effect immediately and knocks a man out. It is the maulers—the Marcianos, the Joe Fraziers, the Henry Armstrongs—the fighters who are hard hitters, but hit without snap, who loosen a man's thinking apparatus from its moorings. Snappy, lightning-like punchers like Joe Louis, Ray Robinson, Charley Burley, Lloyd Marshall, Sam Langford and Benny Deathpane, who scored fifteen one-round knockouts, could put a person out of his misery in a hurry without any permanent damage to his brain. I had caught Morrow on the ropes in the tenth, and after hitting him in the body with a right, I followed with a left uppercut that fairly whistled. Morrow fell straight back and his head hit outside the bottom ropes against the scantily padded ring apron with a thud, and I knew that he was hurt bad. He was in the hospital for five days in a semiconscious state. I visited him and held his hand at bedside, hoping he would soon recover enough to be out of danger and go home. He recovered, all right, and today Len Morrow is a preacher and expounds the Gospel. He boxed only a few times after our match, but he was never able to recapture the quick reflexes and powerful fists he once possessed. This hurting of Morrow was not purposeful on my part as some people would have you believe. This is one of the risks a man takes when he enters professional boxing. There was no intention on my part to hurt him, regardless of the stories about a grudge match because of his knocking me out in our first fight.

TWENTY

●

I am often asked about managers, and I must say first off
that just like in anything else, there are good guys and
bad guys among managers, and like most fighters in my
day and time, I've had some of each. The bad guys I
didn't think much of because of their greed, their ethics
and their unkind, inhuman treatment of their fighters.
They were looking out after themselves and cared little
or nothing about their fighters. Watching almost every
amateur tournament are leeches trying to find potential
breadwinners. And it's not new. This is something that
goes back to the Roman days, when men battered each
other's brains out with iron cestuses that were fitted
around the knuckles. They fought until somebody
dropped, then the winner was matched with other gladiators. This is, I suppose, where the word "gladiator" comes
from—the old Roman days. But boxing has come a long
way since that time, and so have the managers. Managers
have become legitimate businessmen, wearing silk suits
and carrying attaché cases. There are organizations like
the corporation that holds fighters like Joe Frazier, and
there are even some women on the board of directors.
These are legitimate enterprises headed by people who
believe in the physical and mental as well as financial

welfare of their fighters. Unfortunately, there are still some of the old type still around, but I feel that they will disappear, because bad management can send a good fighter down the drain in a hurry. And a fighter can do without this kind of thing, you know, because so many youths who try to make a go of fighting are underprivileged boys who have the guts to get up off the ghetto floor. There are hundreds of thousands that die on the ghetto floor. But the ghetto provides many gladiators who are determined to see the other side of the tracks, to see what it is like to live in a $250-a-month apartment, to have maid service, to taste a chateaubriand now and then, to buy a $7,000 sports car.

Of course, there are many managers much unlike the 50–50 managers, with the expenses coming off the top, who deal honestly and squarely with their fighter. There were and are many great managers who were beautiful guys and gave their fighters a fair and honest deal—like Pop Foster, who managed champion Jimmy McLarnin in the Barney Ross era, and Ancil Hoffman of Sacramento, who guarded and guided the fortunes of Max Baer. To this day Mrs. Mary Baer receives a sizable monthly annuity that was set up for Max Baer by Hoffman. And there is Cal Thompson, a beautiful guy who managed me at a time when I was discouraged because I was getting nowhere. This is the type of man I would have loved to have for a father. What a beautiful man.

People close to fighters—closer even than managers—are the trainers. Not enough can be said about the value to a fighter of a faithful trainer. A Hiawatha Grey to an Archie Moore; a Charley Goldman to a Rocky Marciano; Pop Foster to Jimmy McLarnin; Jack Hurley to Harry Matthews; a Dick Saddler to Charley Shanks and George Foreman.

Practically every fighter has someone who helped him when he was young and needed it most; and one was Mrs. Hester James, mother of one of my boyhood friends, Arthur "Knox" James, who was my buddy in the Missouri Training School for Boys. Mrs. James, one of *the* beautiful women in the world and a real soul sister, understood how a young person felt, not having proper shoes and clothing to wear, and she gave me an opportunity to work and earn enough money to buy clothing during the Depression. Her word was her bond. There have been only a few women in my life, and I would have to include Mrs. James along with my mother, my auntie and my wife, Joan.

But to continue with my fight career. After a so-so year in 1948 I buckled down to business in 1949 and won 12 out of 13 fights, my only loss coming on a foul against Clint Bacon. Of my 12 wins, 10 were by knockouts, and against top men including Bob Satterfield, Jimmy Bivins, the Alabama Kid, and Bob Sikes, and I decisioned Harold Johnson in ten rounds. But in spite of all this I was still unable to get a championship fight and couldn't help but feel discouraged. In 1950 I had only two fights, both of which I won.

However, I still wanted the championship and felt that inactivity and sulking would not get it for me, that this was a negative attitude, so I decided on a positive course of fighting often and against the best in the business. I felt that by doing well I could force a championship match, which I was confident I would win. So in 1951 I had 18 bouts, winning 14 by knockouts, 2 by decisions, had 1 draw and lost only to Harold Johnson on a decision. I had defeated Johnson a few months earlier, and I defeated him again in a rematch early in 1952.

Several of my bouts in 1951 were during a South-

American tour, a land I like very much because of the friendliness of the people and the lack of racial discrimination. It was like a wonderland, and I went as part of a Johnston entourage with Sandy Saddler in 1951. I had a contract to go for one fight with Abel Cestak, a heavyweight who was of Samson-like proportions—huge, tremendous shoulders, huge torso, legs like pillars, beautiful biceps and curly black hair and a face that was fiercely handsome. He was not a great fighter, but he was tough and game, and Juan Peron, who was the President of Argentina, and his wife, Eva, were sitting at ringside. I showered and splattered Cestak's blood over Peron and caused his wife to hide her face and shriek, you know. Afterward Mr. Peron sent word that he would like to meet me in the capital in the Casa Rosada, and he told me that I was the greatest fighter he had ever seen and that he had been a light-heavyweight amateur champion in Buenos Aires himself during the time of his youth. He had fought with many sailors from the American boats, and he thought that I was quite a fighter, and he asked me why I wasn't the light-heavyweight champion of the world. I told him it was politics that was preventing me from getting these fights, and he said, "Are you in politics? *Yo entiendo!*" In Spanish this means "I understand," and no doubt he did understand about politics, so he wished me well and told me that if there was anything I needed in Argentina to call on him.

He made a luncheon engagement for me the following Sunday to go up the Parana River on his yacht. And so I went up with him on this big yacht with a group, including a young lady I had met there and my South-American agent, Roberto D'Angelo, a dear friend. After passing several small towns on this yacht, all I was doing was to come out and wave my hands at the groups of people that

were standing on shore, and they would wave back and I
didn't know that Peron was campaigning then, you see,
but if the saying is true about one picture being worth a
thousand words, then I must have said many a word, because Peron invited me to a lot of places. I went out to a
lot of places where he was, and I went to one political
rally where they were all drinking wine out of a goat bag
and the President and everybody was drinking one right
after the other, so I didn't know what to do, as I didn't
drink. When they gave me the bag I would squeeze a little wine in my mouth, you know, and I'd spit it out the
first chance I'd get when the scene would turn away from
me, because I don't like the taste of liquors or wine of any
kind.

Another place he invited me to was a theater in town,
and he sat on the balcony on one side and I sat on the
other side, and they threw a spotlight on him. Then he
pointed toward where I was and they threw the spotlight
on me. He gave me a gold watch that I wear sometimes—
it keeps the time and the date. It's a beautiful Swiss
watch and is engraved, and he made me feel like a man—
like a real man. I felt that if there ever was a country that
I'd like to establish myself in outside of America, I would
like to give all I had right here because the people
seemed to be so nice, but I had to go back home, and
when I went back home I had $9,000 in my pocket from
this fight and some exhibitions.

I gave a friend of mine nearly 100,000 pesos for his
own investments there and enjoyed myself all the time I
was in Argentina. The rate of exchange spelled 32 pesos
for one American dollar at that time in 1951, and since I
was making about 10,000 pesos for exhibitions each night,
I was considered to be a rich man there. And I suppose I
was a rich man if I had lived there, and I was rich in

friends. There was a little boy named Adolfo Batto, who lived in a little place called Sunchales, and this is a little town, a little area that the United States Army in World War II received most of their imported butter fats from. You see, Argentina is extra rich in dairy products, and Sunchales is a place where chocolates are made, and this little boy lived in a hovel with his mother and the rest of his family. I went to the school, meeting youngsters and practicing my ABC program, and I loved these youngsters, and this teacher asked for some of the best dancers to do a dance for me, a native dance. This was beautiful, and Adolfo came out, but he was reluctant to dance, as his shoes had holes in the soles and the toes were kicked out. But I got him to dance, and he danced beautifully. And I told the teacher to have him come over to my hotel during the noon hour. He came over, and he and Roberto D'Angelo and I took him to a tailor shop. The shop was actually closed, as is their custom for siesta time, which is from twelve till two. So I knocked on the shutter door and the man peeked out and saw who I was and opened the door. I bought the boy two suits of clothes, a pair of beautiful shoes, a tie and two shirts and some underwear. Then I had the man wrap it up and gave him another 100 pesos to send the boy to the dentist because his teeth were in bad condition. I thought with his teeth fixed up he would look better and the 100 pesos was enough because the wage for the average worker there was 300 pesos a week. Adolfo and I corresponded for many years. And whenever I'd run into boys who were in need like Adolfo, I'd help them out with their needs. Somehow or other this got back to Peron, he knew about what I was doing and about my efforts, so he asked me to stay in his country and be one of his ministers in the youth field—in his youth program. I had given it deep consideration, but I had to come back and pursue the light-heavyweight championship, so I told Peron that when I achieved that goal and then won the heavyweight title and held two championships I would feel like I had fulfilled my aspirations in the fistic world. And I told him that when I accomplished these things I would consider being his minister over the welfare of children in Argentina, but it never happened. Peron was kicked out of office and had to go into exile in Madrid, Spain. We have written to each other, and the last letter I got from him was a few months ago—it was a handwritten letter and was very warm, and I feel that this is really a document that I want to keep along with my souvenirs.

I saw nothing wrong in being friendly to Juan and Eva Peron. In fact, I felt it prudent for me as an American to accept an invitation from the head of a foreign government. I neither agreed nor disagreed with Peron's politics. I just never gave them a thought, as I was not politically minded at that time and was only vaguely aware that for some reason the United States did not agree with his policies. I did know that Juan and Eva Peron were friends of the poor, the *descamisados*, or "Shirtless Ones," as they were known, and they did much to help these people and bridge the huge economic gap that existed between the rich and the poor of Argentina. They also loved children, and they treated me like a man— which is more than I can say for a lot of people. In 1952, Eva Peron and Eleanor Roosevelt were named the two most important women in the world by Donald Robinson in his book "The One Hundred Most Important People in the World."

Other personalities such as Jack Dempsey, Sandy Sad-

dler and Charley Johnston met Peron, but somehow it
was Archie Moore who was called on the carpet and criti-
cized by the State Department.

Be that as it may, it was while I was in Argentina that I
received the word that at long last a title fight was set for
me against Joey Maxim. I returned home, and in 1952 I
beat Harold Johnson, Jimmy Slade, Bob Dunlap, Clar-
ence Henry and Clint Bacon before taking on Maxim,
which I did on December 17, 1952. It's hard to describe
my feelings when I fought Maxim for the championship.
In a way it was almost anti-climactic, you know, because
when I received the word that I was to fight him, *that*
was really the climax. I was sure I would win, and yet I
wasn't sure. It's like a student who is about to take an important examination. He is confident that he will pass,
but he isn't sure, because he's not certain what questions
will be thrown at him. Well, that was the way I felt about
Maxim. If he fought the way I thought he would, I knew
I could beat him if I didn't get careless. Any fighter can
be knocked out if hit hard enough in the right place, and
there was always that possibility against a first-class opponent like Maxim. So while I was sure I would win, yet I
wasn't sure. Anything could happen in a fight, and if I
blew this one I knew that after all my yakking I probably
would never again get a chance.

But I won the championship with a clear victory over
Maxim on a fifteen-round decision. I received only $800
for this fight, out of which I had to pay my sparring partners, leaving me with little to show financially for becoming the light-heavyweight champion of the world, while
Maxim received a $100,000 guarantee. But I was sat-
isfied. I had achieved my goal, and I felt that eventually
the championship had to bring me financial rewards. I
was happy and proud after beating Maxim, but at first I

had a hard time convincing myself that it was true. I had been waiting so long for this that I had to pinch myself to make sure I wasn't dreaming. The morning after the fight I bought the newspapers and read about it and I sat there grinning like an idiot as I read that Archie Moore was the light-heavyweight champion of the world, and I guess this has to rate as one of my greatest thrills. Anticipation and frustration increases the joy of an accomplishment, and I sure went through plenty of both before I finally came into possession of the title.

After winning the championship I fought six fights in 1953 and won them all, five by knockouts. Then I fought Maxim in a return match on June 24 and again defeated him in a fifteen-round decision. I then went on another South-American tour, and this time I was even more popular than ever, because I was now the champion, and I won both my matches. It was while on this tour that another match had been set with Maxim for January 27, 1954, in Miami, Florida. Again I defeated Maxim in fifteen rounds, and this was the most satisfying of the Maxim bouts to me, as I knocked him down twice, a feat which I had been unable to do in our two previous fights. I had three more fights that year, scoring kayo wins over Bob Baker, Bert Whitehurst and Harold Johnson.

Shortly after my title defense against Johnson, I was scheduled for a fight in San Diego, but the commission doctor wouldn't let me fight, telling me that I had a heart problem. It was almost a year before I was able to fight again. I had a palpitation in my heart, or uneven beat, and the doctor explained that while this in itself was not dangerous, if not taken care of it could lead to fatal complications, so I went to the hospital and took treatments, and finally I was okay. I was then matched against big Nino Valdes in Las Vegas. This man was big, rough and rugged, so it was a real good test for my heart. I went the full fifteen rounds with him, winning a clear-cut decision.

I then fought tough Bobo Olson in New York on June 22, 1955, with my championship at stake, and I had to take off over twenty pounds in slightly more than a month to make the weight, as when I fought Valdes on May 2, I was very close to 200 pounds. But I made it by using a few of the secrets I had learned along the way and knocked Olson out in the third round. This victory, plus my long and hard letter-writing campaign, earned me a crack at the heavyweight championship against Rocky Marciano, and since I have already described that fight in detail, I will only repeat that Marciano placed a kayo on me in the ninth round after I had decked him in the second in one of the most exciting fights I have ever participated in. I had come within seconds of becoming the heavyweight champion, but close only counts in horseshoes.

In 1956 I had 12 fights and 1 exhibition, winning 8 by knockouts and 3 by decisions. My only loss was a knockout at the hands of Floyd Patterson for the heavyweight championship, which was vacated when Rocky Marciano retired after his fight with me. I don't know if he was joking or not, but when Rocky retired after fighting me, he had said, "If an old man like Archie Moore can give me that much trouble, it's time I got out of boxing." Rocky was a great guy. But back to the Patterson fight. I had always been a favorite with sportswriters, not only because of my fighting ability but because they knew that I was their friend and because I was good copy. But after my defeat by Patterson, many of them turned against me, and this hurt me more than anything else. One writer had said, "Twenty years of fighting have drained Archie Moore. Whatever he had is gone forever."

There were extenuating circumstances regarding my showing against Patterson. I'm not trying to alibi my dismal showing. I'm just stating the facts, which I think the public has a right to know, and they can judge my performance in the light of these facts. But I hope they will be fair and remember some of my other fights when they are judging. First of all, I want to say that I wasn't afraid of Patterson. I never feared any of my opponents. I know I'm as human as anyone else, and I have fears like anyone else, but I've never been afraid of a man. A lot of professional fighters ask me this, and I give them the same answer. I guess it's because I have this unusual ability to hit hard. Even when I was a little boy I used to knock guys down. I knew I could punch, and I wasn't afraid. As a youngster I was kind of withdrawn, but I wouldn't run from anybody.

When I went into the ring I felt excitement, tenseness. The adrenaline would start flowing, and I was raring to go, all keyed up. Yet, I kept my thinking calm. I would plan a fight according to my opponent, his abilities and his style. Every movement I made was carefully calculated and planned, including staring down and fiercely glaring at my opponent during the referee's instructions. There was a little psychological advantage in this, and I always wanted everything going for me, and even during the heat of battle I usually managed to keep my thinking organized and follow my battle plan.

It's a funny thing, but once you get into the ring and start swapping leather with some guy, you know, the adrenaline really starts flowing and insulates you against the pain. Between rounds you sometimes start hurting, you understand, but the pain goes away as soon as you start fighting again, and many times you don't feel the pain until after the fight is over. When you do feel the pain during a fight, it's a sure sign that something is wrong. And there were plenty of things wrong in my life just about that time. I was the victim of a vicious blackmailer's scheme, although I had never been blackmailed before, and I guess I did the wrong thing by paying $15,000, because once you start paying you never finish. But I had been given some bad advice, because I was told that if I brought this thing out in the open my reputation would be damaged and I might have to give up my championship. This proved to be wrong, because when I met the thing head-on and hired an attorney and challenged these people, I found that the blackmailer fled, you see. But in the meantime, when I fought Patterson, this thing hadn't been resolved, and I didn't feel right. Besides the blackmail thing I had financial problems, and I was worried and stale. When I climbed into the ring I didn't even feel like it was me in there. I felt like I was a spectator watching the whole thing.

Patterson is a nice guy and a fine fighter, and he beat me fair and square, and I don't want to take anything away from him, but I honestly feel that I could have beaten him if this strange lethargy hadn't come over me. The usual high spirits that accompanied me in the ring before and during a fight were missing. I knew I was off because I felt every punch that Patterson hit me with. They hurt. I didn't feel the usual excitement and tension. Instead I felt pain, and Patterson isn't the hardest puncher I ever fought. I had been hit much harder by Rocky Marciano and still hadn't felt the pain nearly as much as when I fought Patterson. It's a hard thing to explain, but any fighter will tell you that it has happened to him at one time or another.

But like I said, the barbs of the sportswriters hurt. They hurt me even more than Patterson's punches, and after a bit of brooding I set out to prove that they were wrong about me. My pride had been hurt, and the next year I had six fights, winning them all, one being a championship match with Tony Anthony, whom I disposed of in seven rounds. Through? Not me. Not by a long shot, for I was yet to show the world one of the best and most thrilling fights of my career—one that was to be talked about for years to come, a fight that excited the fans and inspired other boxers probably as much as any of the most famous fights in boxing history.

It was 1958 and I had already been in 9 fights, winning 8 and drawing 1. Then I was matched against Yvon Durelle, with my light-heavyweight championship at stake. Earlier in this book I related just what happened in that fight, but to recap, I was down four times in the early rounds, then came back to knock Durelle out in the eleventh. This, I felt, was my finest hour. I was named Fighter of the Year and awarded the Edward J. Neil Trophy, which was awarded by the Boxing Writers' Association, and it was very satisfying to be back in the good graces of the sportswriters. This fight also enabled me to set a new world's record for knockouts, a record that I feel will stand for a long time. And all this at an age when most fighters were long gone from the ring—sitting in their creaky rocking chairs, reading their scrapbooks, telling fight stories to their children or grandchildren, or anybody else willing to listen; or perhaps running a restaurant or nightclub. That is for the more fortunate ones. Many others, sadly enough, their money gone, exist by doing menial jobs, their former prowess forgotten.

TWENTY-ONE

●

One of the sportswriters who stuck with me through thick and thin is Jack Murphy, illustrious sports editor of the *San Diego Union-Tribune*. He wrote the following article on December 12, 1958, immediately after the Durelle fight and has kindly consented to allow me to use it in this book. It reads:

> Even the critics now agree that Archie is not a con man. After nearly a quarter-century of fighting in tank towns and eating in greasy spoons, Archie Moore is finally getting the recognition and popularity he so richly deserves. In the aftermath of his spectacular brawl with Yvon Durelle, a lot of people have suddenly discovered that Moore isn't just a swaggering old con man engaged in a harmless shell game with the public. There is a new appreciation for his exceptional fighting skills and an admiration bordering on awe for his courage.
>
> This was a fight that revealed what some of us have been saying for quite a spell. Moore is a fighter for the ages. The Mongoose observes a birthday tomorrow—pick a number between 42 and 49, and I can't think of a nicer present than

the prestige he acquired in getting off the floor four times to flatten Durelle in the most exciting fight of the electronic age. This was a fight that did more for child Arch than any single event or combination of events in his long and varied career—possibly even he is unaware of what this enthralling show did for him.

It was a fight that for the first time earned him the sympathy and affection of the public. Instead of bravado and bluster, they saw the more basic qualities of a great fighting heart and craftsmanship of the highest order. Moore's rousing battle came across with such emotional impact that a lot of people began thinking in terms of a demonstration to welcome him home. I don't know if the same thought has occurred to the mayor or chamber of commerce, but it's a subject that deserves consideration and fast action. This was a touch of class for boxing.

The old champ will cash in on his new popularity by taking a bow on the Ed Sullivan television show Sunday night, and probably will return to San Diego on Monday or Tuesday. I don't know if he'll be outfitted with tux, top hat, and gold-headed cane, but you can be sure he'll arrive in style. Moore, incidentally, has an interesting explanation of why he was formally attired at the official weigh-in Wednesday noon. "I'm trying to give boxing a touch of class," he said. "The game needs dignity. Why, Durelle came to the weigh-in dressed like a farmer."

I talked with Moore by phone late in the night, long after the furor had quieted and backslappers had gone their separate ways. He sounded tired, old tired, and his voice was husky with a nagging cold. "Was it a good action show?" he asked, like an actor impatient for the reviews. I assured him that he'd been the star of one of boxing's most exciting dramas. Certainly the wildest and most wonderful fight ever seen on home television screens.

"I'm glad I gave them a good show," he said proudly. "At my age, and this stage of the game, I just had to win. A man has to have drive. He has to have determination to keep going. I had to win for so many reasons. I wasn't fighting just for myself, but for a lot of other people. When I was on the floor I thought about my wife Joan, my daughter Rena, and the baby we're expecting in February. I hope the baby will be a boy. Durelle knocked me down, and I never heard so many people yelling in all my life. I was wondering why those Canadians wouldn't be quiet so I could hear the count. The Canadians are real fans, and Durelle is a dangerous fighter. I underestimated his punch. He hits awful hard. I was lying there and I told myself that this was no place to be resting. And that I better get up and get with it. It seemed like every time I looked up I looked up into referee Jack Sharkey's face, and I got tired of looking at that man. First of all, I thought about ducking. I wanted to make Durelle miss that next punch. I was dazed, but I wasn't hurt. At the end of the round the cobwebs started to clear."

The champion paused as though to gather strength for conversation. "You understand," he said, "there is a tremendous load on my shoulders. So many people depend on me, and I couldn't let them down. The title is all I've got left. I just couldn't give it up."

Moore saved his most precious possession partly on instinct, partly on animal desperation, and largely because he is a superb fighter—a superb fighting man at 175 pounds. Even in his forties, the Mongoose is the best fighter in the world when he trains down to 175 or 180 pounds. With the fat removed, he's fast and deadly. His punching demonstration in the tenth round against Durelle was one of the most brilliantly conceived and executed attacks I've ever witnessed. If Moore would in fact fight Patterson at 180 to 182 pounds, I'm convinced that he would flatten the heavyweight champion inside of ten rounds. Maybe he'll do that one of these years. Say around 1975?"

Jack Murphy is a great guy and a great newspaperman. He tells it like it is. Perhaps he was right and I should have trained down to 180 or 182 for my heavyweight fights. Maybe I would have won the heavyweight championship at that weight.

I have always regretted not having fought Sugar Ray Robinson, and we would have fought if he had agreed to the terms I felt were quite fair. What happened was that I was at his house one evening with my wife, Joan, and we had a nice New Orleans Shrimp à la Creole dinner, and after dinner Ray said he wanted to talk to me. I had a pretty good idea what it was about, because I had heard rumors around town, but I played it dumb. So we left the girls and went to another room, and I said, "Okay, Walker. What's on your mind?" His real name was Walker Smith, Jr., but it bugged him when I called him that or used big words with him, and he gave me a dirty look, but when I started laughing he kind of feebly grinned back at me. He really wasn't in much of a mood for clowning, as he had some big and serious business to discuss.

"Hey, Archie," he began without any preliminaries, "how would you like to fight me?"

This was something I had wanted to do for quite some time, but I played it cool. I knew what was in the air, and I knew just what I wanted.

"Wouldn't mind," I said nonchalantly.

"We'd draw real big," Ray went on.

"No doubt," I replied. "What would be in it for me?"

"A guaranteed half-a-million," Ray replied, expecting me to be stunned by this amount, but I acted like he had said maybe $1,000. I wanted this fight because I knew we could put on a really spectacular fight and probably set a world record in box-office attendance.

"Not bad," I mused. "Tell me more, Raymond."

"Well," he went on, a bit surprised at my regarding the half-million-dollar purse so lightly, "we would be fighting for your title."

"Naturally," I said. I knew that Ray was overweight to fight in the middleweight division, and I would have had a tough time getting down to that weight, so it would have to be for my title, which was a weight that both of us could make. Although I wanted to fight Ray very much, I had a little plan regarding the financial end, so I didn't want to act too eager.

"Well?" Ray asked impatiently. "What about it?"

I had heard that the newly formed theater television was involved in this, but Ray hadn't mentioned this to me. "What about the theater television?" I asked him.

I could see that Ray was getting a bit aggravated. "That's included in the half-million you get," he said.

"I understand that," I came back. "The price is right, Ray. But inasmuch as we can't walk away with that half-

THE ARCHIE MOORE STORY

million each, why don't we work out a deal with those people where we could each invest $250,000 of our purse in the theater television? This would set us up economic-wise for life."

"They won't do it! They won't do it!" Ray said flatly.

Well, I was surprised that Ray could answer my question before he had even discussed it with the people. How did he know what they would or wouldn't do? This was the first time it had been proposed to him, and he tells me flat out that they wouldn't go for it. Well, I didn't like that, so I accepted an offer of $250,000 to fight a re-match with Durelle instead of waiting around on Robin-son. This kind of made Ray mad, but if he would have at least talked to the theater-television people about this and given them my proposition, I would have gone for the deal even if they had refused. I just didn't like the idea of his flat refusal to even approach them with my proposition. And so that is why I never fought Sugar Ray, and I'm sorry about that because I think that we could have made boxing history. I felt sure that I could have beaten him, and he probably felt the same way about me, and that's the way he should have felt. If he had taken up my suggestion and the television people had gone for my idea, we both could have been rich men today. But any-way, I still like Ray Robinson. I think he's a great guy and a great boxer.

Well, so much for the almost-was Ray Robinson-Moore spectacular. On August 12, 1959, I again fought Yvon Durelle, and this time he gave me no problems and I dis-posed of him in three action-packed rounds. He was game, and I had to hit him hard and often in order to beat him.

In 1960 I was signed to fight Erich Schoeppner, the German champion, but the bout was canceled when I broke my wrist in training. On May 25, 1960, I fought tough Willi Besmanoff in Indianapolis, and kayoed him in ten. Then I fought George Abinet in Dallas on September 13 and kayoed him in four. My next fight was a non-title bout against Giulio Rinaldi in Rome, and I dropped a ten-round decision to him. On November 28 I decisioned Buddy Turman in ten rounds in Dallas, and then on March 25, 1961, I again fought Buddy, but this time in Manila, and again I decisioned him in ten. On May 8, I fought a four-round exhibition with Dave Furch in Tucson, then kayoed Cliff Gray in four rounds in Nogales.

About this time the commission was after me to defend my title, so I fought Giulio Rinaldi in a title defense in New York on June 10, 1961. This was the time that everybody said I was too old and too fat, but I trained hard and made the weight, and I went fifteen rounds with Rinaldi, beating him soundly and successfully defending my title. On October 23, 1961, I placed a kayo on Pete Rademacher in six rounds in Baltimore.

My fight career was now drawing to a close. In 1962 I kayoed Alejandro Lavorante in ten, Howard King in one, drew with Willie Pastrano, then, in one of the final fights of my career, lost to Muhammad Ali, the man who was born as Cassius Clay and was destined to be one of the great, though controversial, heavyweight champions. I had groomed him as a young fighter, and now it was a case where the skillful young pupil defeated his aging master. It seemed quite fitting that my fight career should end this way—age finally giving way to youth.

Quite often a boxer who has been around as much as I have is asked who his favorite fighters are. Well, this is a tough question, as there are so many good ones, but I'll take a stab at it. As far as heavyweights go, Jack Johnson stands out in my mind as number one, closely followed by Joe Louis and Jack Dempsey.

Among the light-heavyweights I felt that John Henry Lewis, a good boxer and crisp puncher, was outstanding. In all modesty, I must admit that I feel that Archie Moore ranked up there with the best. A man most of you probably haven't heard of by the name of Alan Mathews, who is out of St. Louis, is my favorite middleweight. And, of course, among the welterweights, the great Sugar Ray Robinson is probably everybody's choice. And he deserves it. The lightweights are a little tough, but I feel that Joe Gans shaded popular Benny Leonard, and this pair is closely followed by Barney Ross, Jimmy McLarnin and Tony Canzoneri. In the featherweight division, Sandy Saddler stands out as tops in my mind, closely followed by Willie Pep. In the bantamweight division, I have to go with six-foot, lanky Al Brown, a Panamanian with a heavy punch. And in the flyweight division my choice is Pancho Villa, closely followed by an Englishman by the name of Jimmy Wilde.

In present-day boxing there is a young bantam by the name of Ruben Olivares, a knockout artist who is making a bid to rise to fistic greatness. And in the heavyweight division I look for a young ex-marine by the name of Mac Foster to become one of the great heavyweights of our time.

I look back on my ring career with considerable nostalgia. For twenty-eight years it had been my life, and now even the tough times are fond memories. The hungry days, and the cheap foods of the past, make the good foods I eat today even more delicious. The hovels I once stayed in make my present home more like a palace. I think back to some of my tougher fights—like Ron Rich-

ards, Charley Burley, Jack Chase, Eddie Booker, Shorty
Hogue, Joey Maxim, Rocky Marciano, Floyd Patterson
and Yvon Durelle—and I feel proud of the record I have
left behind, not so much for the record itself, but because
I know that I have always done the best I could. I recall
the determined feeling I had to do better the next time
when I lost, and the wonderful feeling I had when I won,
the applause of the fans, the congratulations of close
friends. I have bad times to compare with the good times.
After all, if you haven't had any bad times, how can you
appreciate the good ones? I had plenty of bumps along
the way, but plenty of laughs too. Laughs like after the
Durelle fight when my good friend from way back, come-
dian Redd Foxx, had all the hair shaved off the top of his
head except for an *M* for "Moore" after my defeat of Durelle in Canada. Like the time I was hired to be a "fourth
chef" on the railroad, not knowing this was train lingo for
a dishwasher. And so many other memories, like the
many hours spent working out in sweat-and-leather-
smelling gyms, and traveling to Australia, England, Ger-
many, South America and so many other places.

The boxing game has been fun in spite of the hardships
and heartbreaks, and it has been exciting, but all things
must come to an end, and I find what I am doing now is
even more exciting and gratifying, because now, among
other things, I am helping the young, and that is where it
all begins. I am trying to teach right from wrong, and I
may help some youngster who will one day be the first
man on Mars, or become the President of the United
States. Maybe this is too much to look for, but I know
that I will have guided them on the right path to becoming respectable, productive citizens.

Being champion is something I wouldn't have wanted

to miss, but when I was champion I didn't know if some people were my friends because of that or because of me, but now I know people are my friends because they want to help me to help humanity. And humanity needs so much help in so many areas.

I'm as happy as anyone can possibly be considering what is going on in the world today. I have my wonderful wife and family; I have made my peace with the Almighty; and I love the work that I am doing. Besides my youth work, civil rights work, etc., I write an occasional column for Mickey Herkowitz' *Jock* magazine and write a syndicated weekly boxing column for an overseas group. So I manage to pick up a buck here and there. My good friend Dave Gregg out of Joplin, Missouri, used to assist me with my writing, but lately my good "write" arm, Lenny Pearl, has been assisting me with these things.

I am strongly for civil rights. What black man in his right mind wouldn't be? And one has only to attend any of my lectures to discover this. And the only way I may differ from some of my fellow blacks who want the same thing is that I want to see civil rights come about without violence.

I think that Chief Joseph of the Nez Perce Indian Tribe summed up pretty much what I am looking for regarding civil rights. In 1879 he and eight hundred of his people had been captured after a 1,000-mile retreat. He was not bitter, and he showed a pride and knowledge that could stand our nation in good stead today when he stated:

> I know that my race must change. We cannot hold our own with the white men as we are. We only ask an even chance to live as other men live. We ask to be recognized as men. We ask

that the same law shall work alike on all men.

Let me be a free man—free to travel, free to stop, free to work, free to trade, free to choose my own teacher, free to follow the religion of my fathers, free to think and talk and act for myself—and I will obey every law, or submit to the penalty. . . .

And isn't this what Martin Luther King wanted for *all* men? Isn't this what he died for?

That is why I say that I am as happy as a man can be under the existing circumstances. I am doing what I can to bring about civil rights, to help the young and the old, to erase poverty, war and civil unrest, and then, when I see all these things come about, then, and only then, will I be able to say that I am *the* happiest man in the world.

I am confident that these things will come about, and that I *will* be the happiest man in the world, because, you see, faith is in my corner.

AFTERWORD
by Leonard Pearl

What makes a man like Archie Moore? A man who dedicates his life to helping others—to building a better America for all of us. Is it inheritance? Is it environment? Is it a combination of both? What is it that drives Archie Moore to work day and night to help the youth of America when he could be taking it easy, capitalizing on the fame that he so deservedly earned? Is it something that developed within him through his own experiences, or is it divinely inspired? Perhaps it is all these things, and I think that after having read this book, you already know the answer.

Many times I am asked what Archie Moore is really like. As a writer, words are the tools of my trade, but I find that mere words are inadequate in describing Archie in much the same sense as words are inadequate in describing a beautiful sunrise. One must be there to fully believe what he is seeing. However, difficult as the task may be, I will try to paint the picture with words.

The two words that first come to my mind in describing this human dynamo of a man are "compassion" and "charisma." "Compassion," as defined in the dictionary, is "the deep feeling of sharing the suffering of another in the inclination to give aid or support"; and "charisma" is defined as "a rare quality or power attributed to those persons who have demonstrated an exceptional ability for leadership and for securing the devotion of large numbers of people."

This desire to help others regardless of their color, creed or religion is an absolute obsession with Archie. He simply cannot stand to see anybody hurting, either physically or financially, and in that respect he is a paradox. During his boxing days he was the most violent of men in a most violent sport—as any of his opponents can tell you. He neither asked nor gave any quarter during a fight, but he felt compassion for his opponent after the fight and was concerned about a fallen foe. Outside the ring he was, and still is, a gentle, kind and soft-spoken man. He was always happy to help others, even though there were many times when he had to make great sacrifices both financially and physically to help others. I had personal observation of this during a recent tour made with him to the Garden Grove area. On many occasions I have seen him dig into his pocket to give a youngster $5 or $10 when he felt that the youth was in need of a few dollars. He never made it seem like a donation but always contrived to make it seem like a prize. I have seen him do this to the extent of using all his ready cash so that we had to borrow money to buy gas to get home on.

I remember too one afternoon when I was not feeling too well. Archie looked after me like a mother over her sick child, waiting on me hand and foot. He never went anywhere or accepted any social engagements without including me, and that evening, just because I wasn't feeling well enough to make it, he stayed home too, not leaving me until I felt better.

Archie has always been at his happiest when helping

others. In 1953 he was visiting Miami and heard about a four-year-old girl, Cora Lee Hunter, who was going blind and needed money to finance a corneal transplant. He immediately looked the girl up and gave her some money. But he didn't stop there. He went on television to make pleas for donations to help the girl, appeared in benefits for her and continually dug into his own pocket to help pay for her operations. His pleas paid off and Cora Lee received the needed operations. I don't think anybody could turn Archie down. If he ever wanted a bearskin, I don't think he would have to shoot the animal. He would just talk to him and the bear would take off his hide and beg Archie to take it. Fifteen years later, in 1968, Archie again visited Miami, and one of the thrills of his life was to see and talk to his friend Cora Lee, then grown to a beautiful young lady of nineteen years and gainfully employed.

During his fighting days, Archie never refused an invitation to speak at reform schools and jails and point out to the men that they still could make it on the outside. But donations and lectures were not the only ways in which Archie tried to help people. Sometimes it would be a one-line bit of advice, or perhaps a bit of humor to make a fallen opponent feel better.

One of the many men who benefited by Archie's sage advice was John Schaff. It was back in 1953 when Schaff, a U.S. airman, was training for the Air Force championship bouts in a gym in San Francisco. Archie was training in the same gym and asked Schaff if he would like to spar a few rounds with him. Schaff readily agreed, and although they were just supposed to spar and not do any damage, Schaff decided he would try to get in a good lick whenever he could. He jolted the surprised champ in the first round and Archie cautioned him to take it easy. But

in the third round, Schaff's cockiness got the better of
him and he caught Archie with a hard shot to the head
and set himself to throw a finishing punch, but that was
the last thing he remembered until he woke up in the
dressing room. Archie was bending over him. "What are
your plans for the future?" the champ asked softly.

"Well," Schaff replied, "I thought I might go in for
professional boxing."

"You might make it," Archie said. "But if you didn't,
then what would you do?"

"Oh, I'd go to school and become an athletic director
or coach," Schaff replied.

"Why don't you get your education first and then make
up your mind," Archie advised.

Schaff took Archie's advice and has always been grateful, as he now has a good job as a physical-education specialist.

Another time, George Plimpton, an excellent writer
who believes in living his parts, wanted to box a few
rounds with Archie so he could write about it. Plimpton,
a courageous young man, had played with a pro-football
team, a pro-baseball team and had played against a Davis
Cup tennis champion—just to get firsthand knowledge of
what he was writing about. Archie admired his courage
but was reluctant to box him, as he had everything to lose
and nothing to gain in boxing an amateur. Through his
awkwardness, an amateur can unintentionally hurt an experienced boxer, just as an amateur race driver can cause
a serious accident in a race against pros. However, Archie
finally agreed, deciding he would just defend himself
against Plimpton, as he didn't want to hurt him. Archie
had thought that it would just be a little private affair at
Stillman's Gym, but when he got into the ring he found
that a few hundred of Plimpton's friends were on hand to

see what the writer could do against the champ—and perhaps make a chump out of him. Archie found it an embarrassing experience, yet he didn't want to look bad. He concentrated on defense, but even so, in the course of the match he unintentionally hurt Plimpton a few times. After it was over, Plimpton was sitting on a bench in the dressing room, sick to his stomach and bleeding from his nose. Archie walked over to him and said, "That's okay, champ. You did a real fine job. And don't forget, you're entitled to a rematch."

Plimpton managed a weak grin. The last thing he wanted was to get back in the ring with Archie, but the champ's words of recognition for a game effort made him feel better.

Archie is a strange combination. He is an idealist and dreamer, yet he is a realist. His ideals are high, and he dreams of great things for *all* people in America, yet he is realistic enough to know that these things aren't going to be accomplished easily.

Archie is now in the biggest fight of his life. He's trying for his 141st knockout. The punches he is throwing now will be felt for years to come. They are important and vital in making ours a better country. Archie wants to help the underprivileged; to curb juvenile delinquency; to achieve racial harmony and equality; to erase poverty; to quell civil unrest. He wants to make this a better America. I don't think he realized how big a fight it would turn out to be. But I don't think it would have mattered to him. He would have tackled it anyway. It has been a rough, tough fight so far, and promises to get even tougher before all his goals are reached. And it is taking a lot out of Archie, but I for one am betting that he will come up with the biggest win of his life.

His opposition comes from many directions. There are

the white bigots, who are against him because he is black
and is for civil rights. There are the black extremists, who
feel that nothing short of violence will give them their
rights, and some of these call him an Uncle Tom because
of his nonviolent views and because he counts many
white men among his friends. Some of the opposition
comes from the apathy of politicians and businessmen,
who fail to realize just how great his programs are and
how much they can do to solve our tremendous internal
problems. But, just as he did in the ring, Archie keeps
punching away, and eventually his courage and determination has to bring victory. Archie is a simple yet com-
plex man who has a way of making dreams come true. If
you are black, you will fully understand what Archie is
saying and trying to do in regard to equality for all races
and living together in harmony; and if you are white, try
to imagine yourself as being black—and you too will understand. Nobody, whether black, white, brown, yellow
or red—and of every religious belief—cannot fail to understand the importance of his youth work, because the
youth of today are the men and women who will run our
country tomorrow.

Archie's daily mail looks like a who's who of the world.
On a given day he might receive a letter from the President of the United States or from some kid in South Africa who wants Archie to help him become a boxer. Archie tries to answer all mail, even if it is just a few lines. I
have seen him sit up into the early hours of the morning
answering his mail, and this after having arrived home
following a strenuous lecture tour across the country.

Although there is still a tough road ahead, Archie's
work is beginning to receive recognition and backing. He
loves people and people love him, and he has thousands
of loyal friends. He loves a good laugh and is a super-

charged man of action, and when there is work to be done he keeps everybody hopping. Being human, he has his faults. He can be driving and demanding, but he drives nobody any harder than he drives himself, nor does he demand as much from others as from himself. He is impatient with failure, but more impatient with any of his own than someone else's. On the other hand, he always lauds a job well done, he always seeks to make a person feel important, is quick to forgive error and always seeks recognition for his friends. Whenever I am present at any of his presentations, he never fails to introduce me as a good friend and assistant. The applause of the audience is heartwarming, but the knowledge that Archie Moore thinks enough of me to introduce me is even more gratifying.

Life with Archie Moore is never dull. He is impulsive and impetuous, and on the spur of the moment he might decide to drive from San Diego to Los Angeles, perhaps to buy some kid a punching bag or pair of boxing trunks —or as has happened on more than one occasion when we were rooming together in Santa Ana, I would awaken at three or four in the morning and see Archie off in the corner with a single lamp burning, writing away furiously. Or there were times when he would wake me up in the middle of the night to discuss something he had on his mind.

One day we were driving back to Santa Ana after doing a presentation in Garden Grove when suddenly Archie turned to me and asked, "How would you like to go up to Hollywood with me?"

"Right now?" I asked.

"Sure," he replied. "Some studio has been after me to take a part in a movie, and I'd like you to sit in on the conference."

"Fine," I said. "Let's go." I had never been inside a movie studio and was looking forward to it.

In a couple of hours we were at the studio and ushered into the producer's plush office by a beautiful and efficient secretary. It was a large office with red carpeting and black-leather overstuffed chairs and lounges, and to one side was a long conference table, but dominating the whole scene was a huge desk, in back of which were various memorabilia of different movies this producer had made. The secretary asked us if we would like anything to eat or drink, telling us that the producer was shooting a scene at the moment but would be right with us.

In a very few minutes the producer, a short and heavy-set man, appeared with a couple of his assistants, and we shook hands all around. The secretary handed him a large manila envelope from which he extracted a script.

"Archie," he began, "I have a part just tailormade for you."

Archie nodded. "Tell me about it," he said.

"Well," the producer went on, "it's about an ex-prizefighter. So we need an ex-fighter who can act. From your credits both in boxing and in films, you fill the bill."

"What kind of part is it?" Archie insisted.

The producer held up the script. "You would be more or less of a hermit, living alone out in a shack on the desert. You're sore at the world for the way they used you, and you're a boozer."

Archie held up his hand. "Sorry," he said, "but I don't drink, and I couldn't take the part of a man who does."

The producer thought for a minute. "Archie," he said, "we want you for this part. You're perfect. An ex-fighter who can act. It's a strong supporting role, and if necessary we can cut out the boozer part. How about it?"

"Well," Archie said, "sounds all right. But I would have to read the script first."

"Of course," the producer agreed. "Will a week be enough time?"

"Sure," Archie agreed, taking the script from the producer and handing it to me. We shook hands all around once again and headed back for Santa Ana. "Read it over and let me know what you think about it," Archie said.

I spent the next couple of evenings reading the script, and while it was a very interesting and exciting story, there were some sex and nude scenes in it, although none of this had to do with Archie's part. I reported this to Archie.

He shook his head. "Call them up and tell them I can't do it," he said. Thus does Archie Moore live up to his principles, even though the part would have paid well and come at a time when the money would have come in handy.

Dr. Myron Kirsch, assistant superintendent of the Garden Grove Unified School District, saw the value of Archie's program and was instrumental in having the school board hire him to make a tour of the Garden Grove schools.

Dr. Hilton Bell, who was the superintendent of the school district, had heard of Archie's ABC program and sent a group of educators from the district to San Diego to observe firsthand what he was doing. Dr. Kirsch was quite impressed and liked what he saw, and he sold the school board and its new superintendent, Dr. David Paynter, on the idea of having Archie make his presentations, so he telephoned Archie to come up and negotiate a contract. I went along with him and we agreed upon a satisfactory contract. Archie was to make nineteen ap-

pearances in sixteen days, but this had to be increased to
a backbreaking thirty-five appearances in sixteen days,
due to the fact that most of the school auditoriums could
not hold all the students at one assembly. Archie took the
increase in stride, however, although many days he would
be completely exhausted after doing from two to four
assemblies in one day.

The tour was a complete and huge success, and the
reactions of students, teachers and parents was great. Acceptance was overwhelmingly enthusiastic and very
nearly unanimous. During the thirty-five presentations
before over 20,000 students, only two boys gave Archie
any problems, and both were at a continuation school,
which is where youngsters who have been suspended
from other schools are given a last chance. One of them,
when called on the stage to participate, was asked what
he wanted to be in life. His answer was a surly: "I don't
want to be nothin'." Archie, with the firmness of an um-
pire waving a player out of a ballgame, motioned the boy
off the stage. The other, when called on to sing, said to
Archie, "You sing!"

Archie said, "Okay, I'll sing, I'm not very good, but at
least I'm going to try, and that's all I want you to do—just
try."

Archie sang, and when he finished he received a rousing round of applause. Then the boy who had refused
sang a song. Archie shook his hand. "You see," he told the
boy, "things are never as tough as they seem. All you've
got to do is try, and that's the way it is in life. You never
get anywhere or know if you can do something unless you
try."

Archie is a master at subtly weaving these messages in
with the "games" he has the students play. For example,
when he first introduces himself to the students he has

called up on the stage to participate in the program, he asks to be called Instructor Moore while the game is being played and tells the students that when asked their names, they are to reply, "Student John," "Student Mary," etc. It goes something like this:

Archie will ask: "What is my name?"

The students will answer in a moderate voice: "Instructor Moore."

Archie will raise his voice. "I didn't hear you. *What is my name?*"

The students will speak louder. "Instructor Moore."

Archie shouts: "I still can't hear you! *What is my name?*"

"Instructor Moore!" the students shout back.

Archie breaks into a grin and the students relax. "That's the way I like to hear you," he congratulates them. "I want you to speak up. You young people must speak up and be heard. Our country needs your young voices to be heard if we are to get back on our feet. When you see wrong, speak out! Don't let people burn up your schools. How are you going to learn if you have no schools to go to? And if you don't learn, you'll get nowhere in life. And burning doesn't solve anything. As taxpayers, it only costs your parents money. They have to pay for this destruction. And eventually you'll have to pay for it. So stop wrong whenever and wherever you see it. So you see why I want you to speak out."

Archie is quick to see and take advantage of a current topic to drive home a point. At one of the schools we visited in Garden Grove, he noticed a poster urging students to fight pollution. Archie held up the school poster advocating the anti-pollution drive.

"Yes," he said. "We must all fight pollution. But not only pollution of our air and water but also pollution of the mind and heart. You must drive this pollution out of your minds and hearts. This pollution of hatred, violence and bigotry. And once you do that, you'll be on your way to being better men and women."

And then he will go on with his "game," making it amusing and entertaining, but always driving home his points, just as surely as he drove home his knockout punches in the ring.

Student reaction, except in the two rare cases I mentioned, was very gratifying, and made all the work worthwhile. I observed one little Mexican-American boy who must have been about fourteen years old. His clothes and downcast eyes told the story of a disadvantaged boy from a low-income minority group who probably felt that he had nowhere to go in life beyond being a menial laborer. However, as the program went on and Archie paid particular attention to this boy—as he does when he sees youngsters like this—encouraging him and slyly keeping him in the game, the boy's head was held higher and higher, and at times a smile even crossed his somber face. When it was all over he held himself erect, and there was a bright gleam of hope and determination in his eyes as he shook Archie's hand and said, "I don't know what it's going to be yet, Mr. Moore, but I'm going to be something."

On another occasion I noticed a youngster of no more than fourteen—although he was bigger than Archie—who had been hanging on the fringe of a large group seeking autographs. When all the autographs were signed, the big lad followed us out of the auditorium and finally caught up with us and said, "Mr. Moore, can I shake your hand?"

"Why, certainly son," Archie smiled. "What's your

name?" "Bill . . ." the youth started to say, and suddenly he grimaced and tears spouted from his eyes.

Archie was immediately concerned. "What's the matter, Bill?" he asked. "Don't you feel good?"

"I'm all right," the boy managed. "It's just such a thrill shaking hands and talking with a great man like you. You're doing so much good."

Both Archie and I were moved by the youngster's obvious sincerity. Archie said, "Well, you just dry up those tears and we'll have Mr. Pearl take a picture of us together and I'll send it to you. Okay?"

The boy's smile was warm, and I took their picture, and later Archie autographed it and sent it to the happy boy.

Archie has often challenged an audience to boo him out of the auditorium if they didn't like what he said. It hasn't happened yet, and I don't think it ever will. Almost invariably he receives a standing ovation when he is through. When speaking to youngsters he speaks to them in their own language. He will use terms like "cool it, baby," or "you dig"—words and phrases he doesn't use when addressing an older group, say, at a Rotary Club. At times like this, his use of words is as flawless as that of a college professor. And when he discusses boxing he speaks in the language of the ring.

Archie has many friends who are always willing to help him out materially, and one I met while we were in Anaheim is a fine man by the name of Leonard Robbins, president of a men's clothing-store chain. We met with Robbins, who is an old friend of Archie, and after a bit of small talk, Archie explained what he was doing in the area and asked if Robbins would be willing to donate some clothes for winners in the participation games.

Robbins practically gave Archie a blank check, knowing that he wouldn't take advantage of his generosity. Such are the kind of friends that Archie attracts, and there are many more, and of all colors and creeds.

I recently talked to Mr. Nat Fleischer, president and editor of *Ring Magazine,* and editor and publisher of *The Ring Boxing Encyclopedia and Record Book,* who is known as "Mr. Boxing" and is probably the leading boxing authority in the world. I asked his permission to use Archie's record in this book and he gladly gave his permission. We then discussed Archie for a few minutes, and Mr. Fleischer said, "Archie was one of our leading light-heavyweights and heavyweights, although he fought mostly as a light-heavyweight for a long period. He was a clever fellow, and a good, sound hitter. He had to wait a long time before his ability was recognized by promoters to give him an opportunity to fight for the world's title. If he had not forced the issue through consistent publicity that he himself had sent out, he probably would never have fought for the title. He was a top man in his field for many, many years. There were very few in his division who could match his skill, and he continued to remain on top of the heap for many years."

This was indeed a great accolade from a most knowledgeable man. There is no doubt about it—Archie Moore was a great fighter—a great champion. One of the greatest. But I think that when the final gong sounds for Archie Moore, he will be even better remembered for his greatness as a man. When Archie hung up his gloves, boxing lost a tiger with the heart of a lion and the mind of a fox. But the world has gained a humanitarian with a heart of gold and the mind of a saint.

But the Magnificent Mongoose is still fighting, but now it is not for himself but for others. He is fighting juvenile delinquency, fighting to motivate youngsters to lead better lives and achieve great things, fighting for racial harmony, fighting for a better America, fighting for justice and equality for all, fighting for the right to life, liberty and the pursuit of happiness—*for all.*

In 1968, Archie Moore was named Mr. San Diego by a grateful city. I believe that when the scope and results of his work become better-known he will become a prime candidate for the title of Mr. United States of America.

This information is from Nat Fleischer's *The Ring Boxing Encyclopedia and Record Book*, and is used by permission of Mr. Nat Fleischer.

1936

Jan. 31	Poco Kid, Hot Springs	KO	2
Feb. 7	Dale Richards, Poplar Bluff	KO	1
Feb. 18	Ray Halford, St. Louis	KO	3
Feb. 20	Willie Harper, St. Louis	KO	3
Feb. 21	Courtland Shepard, St. Louis	L	6
	Kneibert Davidson	KO	2
	Ray Brewster	KO	3
	Billy Simms	KO	2
	Johnny Leggs	KO	1
April 15	Peter Urban, Cleveland	KO	6
April 16	Frankie Nelson, Cleveland	L	6
May 4	Tiger Brown, St. Louis	L	6
May 18	Thurman Martin, St. Louis	W	5
	Ferman Burton	KO	1
	Billy Simms	KO	1
July 14	Murray Allen, Quincy, Ill.	KO	6
	Julius Kemp	KO	3
	Four H. Posey	KO	6

Oct. 9	Sammy Jackson, St. Louis	W	6
	Dick Putnam	KO	3
Dec. 8	Sammy Jackson, St. Louis	D	6
	Sammy Christian, St. Louis	KO	6

1937

Jan. 5	Dynamite Payne, St. Louis	KO	1
Jan. 18	Johnny Davis, Quincy, Ill.	KO	3
Feb. 2	Joe Huff, St. Louis	KO	2
	Murray Allen, Keokuk, Ia.	KO	2
April 9	Charley Dawson, Indianapolis	KO	5
April 23	Karl Martin, Indianapolis	KO	1
	Frank Hatfield	KO	1
	Al Dublinsky	KO	1
Aug. 19	Deacon Logan, St. Louis	KO	3
Sept. 9	Sammy Slaughter, Indianapolis	W	10
Nov. 16	Sammy Christian, St. Louis	W	5
	Sammy Jackson	KO	8

1938

Jan. 7	Carl Lautenschlager, St. Louis	KO	2
	Frank Rowsey, San Diego	KO	2
May 20	Jimmy Brent, San Diego	KO	1
May 27	Ray Vargas, San Diego	KO	3
June 24	Johnny Romero, San Diego	L	10
July	Johnny Sikes, San Diego	KO	4
Aug. 5	Lorenzo Pedro, San Diego	W	10
Sept.	Johnny Romero, San Diego	KO	8
Sept. 27	Tom Henry	KO	4
Nov. 22	Ray Lyle, St. Louis	KO	2
Dec. 7	Irish Bob Turner, St. Louis	KO	2
	Bobby Yannes	KO	2

1939

Jan. 20	Jack Moran, St. Louis	KO	1
Mar. 2	Domenic Ceccarelli, St. Louis	KO	1
Apr. 1	Marty Simmons, Minneapolis	W	10
Apr. 20	Teddy Yarosz, St. Louis	L	10
July 21	Jack Coggins, San Diego	NC	8
Sept. 22	Bobby Seaman, San Diego	KO	7
Dec. 7	Honeyboy Jones, St. Louis	W	10
Dec. 21	Shorty Hogue, San Diego	L	6

1940

Mar. 30	Jack McNamee, Melbourne	KO	4
Apr. 18	Ron Richards, Sydney	KO	10
May 9	Atilio Sabatino, Sydney	KO	5
May 12	Joe Delaney, Adelaide	KO	7
June 2	Frank Lindsay, Tasmania	KO	4
June 27	Fred Henneberry, Sydney	KO	7
July 11	Ron Richards, Sydney	W	12
Oct. 18	Pancho Ramierez, San Diego	KO	5
Dec. 5	Shorty Hogue, San Diego	L	6

1941

Jan. 17	Clay Rowan, San Francisco	KO	1
Jan. 31	Shorty Hogue, San Diego	L	10
Feb.	Clay Rowan, San Diego	KO	1
Feb. 26	Eddie Booker, San Diego	D	10
	(Retired because of extended illness)		

1942

Jan. 28	Bobby Britt, Phoenix	KO	3

Feb. 27	Guero Martinez, San Diego	KO	2
Mar. 17	Jimmy Casino, San Francisco	KO	5
Oct. 30	Shorty Hogue, San Diego	KO	2
Nov. 6	Tabby Romero, San Diego	KO	2
Nov. 27	Jack Chase, San Diego	W	10
Dec. 11	Eddie Booker, San Diego	D	10

1943

May 8	Jack Chase, San Diego	W	15
July 28	Eddie Cerda, San Diego	KO	3
Aug.	Big Boy Hogue, Lane Field	KO	5
Aug. 2	Jack Chase, San Francisco	L	15
Aug. 16	Aaron Wade, San Francisco	L	10
Nov. 5	Kid Hermosillo, San Diego	KO	5
Nov. 26	Jack Chase, San Diego	W	10

1944

Jan. 7	Amado Rodriquez, San Diego	KO	1
Jan. 21	Eddie Booker, Hollywood	KO by	8
Mar. 24	Roman Starr, Hollywood	KO	2
Apr. 21	Charles Burley, Hollywood	L	10
May 19	Kenny La Salle, San Diego	W	10
Sept. 1	Battling Monroe, San Diego	KO	6
Dec. 18	Nate Bolden, N.Y.C.	W	10

1945

Jan. 11	Joey Jones, Boston	KO	1
Jan. 29	Bob Jacobs, New York	KO	9
Feb. 12	Nap Mitchell, Boston	KO	6
Apr. 2	Nate Bolden, Baltimore	W	10

Apr. 23   Teddy Randolph, Baltimore...... KO 9
May 21   Lloyd Marshall, Cleveland....... W 10
June 18   George Kochan, Baltimore....... KO 6
June 26   Lloyd Marshall, Cleveland....... KO 10
Aug. 22   Jimmy Bivins, Cleveland....... KO by 6
Sept. 17   Cocoa Kid, Baltimore............. KO 8
Oct. 22   Holman Williams, Baltimore...... L 10
Nov. 12   Odell Riley, Detroit............ KO 6
Nov. 26   Holman Williams, Baltimore...... KO 11
Dec. 13   Colion Chaney, St. Louis......... KO 5

1946

Jan. 28   Curtis Sheppard, Baltimore....... W 12
Feb. 5   Georgie Parks, Washington........ KO 1
May 2   Verne Escoe, Orange............. KO 7
May 20   Ezzard Charles, Pittsburgh....... L 10
Aug. 19   Buddy Walker, Baltimore......... KO 4
Sept. 9   Shamus O'Brien, Baltimore....... KO 2
Oct. 23   Billy Smith, Oakland............. D 12
Nov. 6   Jack Chase, Oakland............. D 10

1947

Mar. 18   Jack Chase, Los Angeles.......... KO 9
Apr. 11   Rusty Payne, San Diego........... W 10
May 5   Ezzard Charles, Cincinnati....... L 10
June 16   Curtis Sheppard, Washington...... W 10
July 14   Bert Lytell, Baltimore.......... W 10
July 30   Bobby Zander, Oakland........... W 12
Sept. 8   Jimmy Bivins, Baltimore.......... KO 9
Nov. 10   George Fitch, Baltimore.......... KO 6

1948

Jan. 13	Ezzard Charles, Cleveland	KO by 8
Apr. 12	Dusty Wilkerson, Baltimore	KO 7
Apr. 19	Doc Williams, Newark	KO 7
May 5	Billy Smith, Cincinnati	W 10
June 2	Leonard Morrow, Oakland	KO by 1
June 28	Jimmy Bivins, Baltimore	W 10
Aug. 2	Ted Lowery, Baltimore	W 10
Sept. 20	Billy Smith, Baltimore	KO 4
Oct. 15	Henry Hall, New Orleans	L 10
Nov. 1	Lloyd Gibson, Wash., D.C.	LF 4
Nov. 15	Henry Hall, Baltimore	W 10
Dec. 6	Bob Amos, Washington	W 10
Dec. 27	Charley Williams, Baltimore	KO 7

1949

Jan. 10	Alabama Kid, Toledo	KO 4
Jan. 31	Bob Satterfield, Toledo	KO 3
Mar. 4	Alabama Kid, Columbus	KO 3
Mar. 23	Dusty Wilkerson, Phila.	KO 6
Apr. 11	Jimmy Bivins, Toledo	KO 8
Apr. 26	Harold Johnson, Philadelphia	W 10
June 13	Clinton Bacon, Indianapolis	LF 6
June 27	Bob Sikes, Indianapolis	KO 3
July 29	Esco Greenwood, No. Adams	KO 2
Oct. 4	Bob Amos, Toledo	W 10
Oct. 24	Phil Muscato, Toledo	KO 6
Dec. 6	Doc Williams, Hartford	KO 8
Dec. 13	Leonard Morrow, Toledo	KO 10

1950

Jan. 31	Bert Lytell, Toledo	W 10
July 31	Vernon Williams, Chicago	KO 2

1951

Jan. 2	Billy Smith, Portland	KO	8
Jan. 28	John Thomas, Panama	KO	1
Feb. 21	Jimmy Bivins, N.Y.	KO	9
Mar. 13	Abel Cestac, Toledo	W	10
Apr. 26	Herman Harris, Flint	KO	4
May 14	Art Henri, Baltimore	KO	4
June 9	Abel Cestac, Buenos Aires	KO	10
June 23	Karel Sys, Buenos Aires	D	10
July 8	Alberto Lovell, Buenos Aires	KO	1
July 15	Vicente Quiroz, Montevideo	KO	6
July 26	Victor Carabajal, Cordoba	KO	3
July 28	Americo Capitanelli, Tucuman	KO	3
Aug. 5	Rafael Miranda, Argentina	KO	4
Aug. 17	Alfredo Lagay, Bahia Blanca	KO	3
Sept. 5	Embrell Davison, Detroit	KO	1
Sept. 24	Harold Johnson, Philadelphia	W	10
Oct. 29	Chubby Wright, St. Louis	KO	7
Dec. 10	Harold Johnson, Milwaukee	L	10

1952

Jan. 29	Harold Johnson, Toledo	W	10
Feb. 27	Jimmy Slade, St. Louis	W	10
May 19	Bob Dunlap, San Francisco	KO	6
June 26	Clarence Henry, Baltimore	W	10
July 25	Clint Bacon, Denver	KO	4
Dec. 17	Joey Maxim, St. Louis	W	15
	(Won World Light-Heavyweight Title)		

1953

Jan. 27	Toxie Hall, Toledo	KO	4
Feb. 16	Leonard Dugan, San Francisco	KO	8

Mar. 3   Sonny Andrews, Sacramento...... KO 5
Mar. 11   Nino Valdes, St. Louis........... W 10
Mar. 17   Al Spaulding, Spokane........... KO 3
Mar. 30   Frank Buford, San Diego......... KO 9
June 24   Joey Maxim, Ogden.............. W 15
          (Title Bout)
Aug. 22   Reinaldo Ansaloni, Buenos Aires.... KO 4
Sept. 12 Dogomar Martinez, Buenos Aires... W 10

1954

Jan. 27   Joey Maxim, Miami.............. W 15
          (Title Bout)
Mar. 9   Bob Baker, Miami Beach.......... KO 9
June 7   Bert Whitehurst, New York........ KO 6
Aug. 11   Harold Johnson, New York........ KO 14
          (Title Bout)

1955

May 2   Nino Valdes, Las Vegas........... W 15
June 22   Bobo Olson, New York............ KO 3
          (World Light-Heavyweight Title Bout)
Sept. 21 Rocky Marciano, New York...... KO by 9
          (For World Heavyweight Title)
Oct. 22   Dale Hall, Philadelphia......... Exh. 4

1956

Feb. 2   Dale Hall, Fresno............... Exh. 4

Feb. 20	Howard King, San Francisco......	W 10
Feb. 27	Bob Dunlap, San Diego..........	KO 1
Mar. 17	Frankie Daniels, Hollywood......	W 10
Mar. 27	Howard King, Sacramento........	W 10
Apr. 10	Willie Bean, Richmond..........	KO 5
Apr. 16	George Parmentier, Seattle.......	KO 3
Apr. 26	Sonny Andrews, Edmonton.......	KO 4
Apr. 30	Gene Thompson, Tucson.........	KO 3
June 5	Yolande Pompey, London........	KO 10
	(Light-Heavyweight Title Bout)	
July 25	James J. Parker, Toronto.........	KO 9
Sept. 8	Roy Shire, Ogden...............	KO 3
Nov. 30	Floyd Patterson, Chicago.......	KO by 5
	(For Vacant World Heavyweight Title)	

1957

May 1	Hans Kalbfell, Essen.............	W 10
June 2	Alain Cherville, Stuttgart.........	KO 6
Sept. 20	Tony Anthony, Los Angeles.......	KO 7
	(World Light-Heavyweight Title Bout)	
Oct. 31	Bob Mitchell, Vancouver..........	KO 5
Nov. 5	Eddie Cotton, Seattle............	W 10
Nov. 29	Roger Rischer, Portland..........	KO 4

1958

Jan. 18	Luis Ignacio, Sao Paulo..........	W 10
Feb. 1	Julio Neves, Rio de Janeiro.......	KO 3
Mar. 4	Bert Whitehurst, San Bernardino...	KO 10
Mar. 10	Bob Albright, Vancouver..........	KO 7
May 2	Willi Besmanoff, Louisville.......	W 10
May 17	Howard King, San Diego..........	W 10

May 26   Charlie Norkus, San Francisco.....   W 10
June 9   Howard King, Sacramento.........   W 10
Aug. 4   Howard King, Reno..............   D 10
Dec. 10 Yvon Durelle, Montreal..........   KO 11
         (World Light-Heavyweight Title)

1959

Feb. 2   Eddie Cotton, Victoria, Can.......   Exh. 5
Mar. 9   Sterling Davis, Odessa...........   KO 3
Aug. 12 Yvon Durelle, Montreal..........   KO 3
         (Title Bout)

1960

May 25   Willi Besmanoff, Indianapolis......   KO 10
         (Non-title)
Sept. 13 George Abinet, Dallas............   KO 4
         (Non-title)
Oct. 29 Giulio Rinaldi, Rome............   L 10
         (Non-title)
Nov. 28 Buddy Turman, Dallas...........   W 10
         (Non-title)
Oct. 25 N.B.A. withdrew recognition from Moore.

1961

Mar. 25 Buddy Turman, Manila...........   W 10
         (Non-title)
May 8   Dave Furch, Tucson.............   Exh. 4
         (Non-title)
May 12   Cliff Gray, Nogales.............   KO 4

June 10   Giulio Rinaldi, New York .... W 15
                   (Title Bout)
Oct. 23   Pete Rademacher, Baltimore .... KO 6
                   (Non-title)

1962

Feb. 10   N.Y. and E.B.U. withdrew
                   recognition from Moore.
Mar. 30   Alejandro Lavorante, Los Angeles .. KO 10
May 7   Howard King, Tijuana .... KO 1
May 28   Willie Pastrano, Los Angeles ...... D 10
Nov. 15   Cassius Clay, Los Angeles .... KO by 4

1963

Mar. 15   Mike DiBiase, Phoenix .... KO 3

Retired in 1964 to enter Cinema and Television Fields.

1965

Aug. 27   Nap Mitchell, Michigan City .. Exh. KO 3

TB	KO	WD	WF	D	LD	LF	KOBY	ND	NC
228	140	53	0	8	17	2	7	0	1